After Midnight

Also by Michael Grumley

Atlantis: The Autobiography of a Search
WITH ROBERT FERRO

There Are Giants in the Earth

Hard Corps
PHOTOGRAPHS BY ED GALLUCCI

After Midnight

Michael Grumley

Drawings by the Author

Charles Scribner's Sons   New York

Text copyright © 1977, 1978 Michael Grumley
Illustrations copyright © 1978 Michael Grumley

Library of Congress Cataloging in Publication Data
Grumley, Michael.
    After midnight.

    1. Labor and laboring classes—United States—Case stud-
ies. I. Title.
HD8072.G86   301.44′42′0926   77-20699
ISBN 0-684-15310-6

1 3 5 7 9 11 13 15 17 19 v|c 20 18 16 14 12 10 8 6 4 2

Printed in the United States of America

My thanks to those whose stories are here included, and to Margaret Sanders Huenergardt, Diane Cleaver, Vicky Jennings, John McCormack, Frances and Oliver Rutledge, and Laurie Graham.

MG

For Robert Ferro

Your night is my day. Outside, it is morning.

Bête: *La Belle et La Bête*

JEAN COCTEAU

Contents

After Midnight

Death and Doctor Goodglass

The attack has been a mild one, a fluttering of the valves on the heart's left side. It is being stressed that such an attack is a warning, an announcement of the body's vulnerability, a plea. The crisis of six hours before has passed. The nurse leaves the room. In the dimness of the hospital room, the objects of apprehension and scrutiny are no longer objects of either. The column of paper cups beside the bed, the single chair covered in green vinyl, the blank television screen; that which has been ominous is now merely familiar. Tension relaxes and is diffused. The figures of the hospital night, orderlies and ambulance drivers and implacable women in white, are again perceived as men and women instead of whispering gods. The patient's life is restored to him, and with the expectation of normalcy comes the reestablishment of proportion and order.

The patient sleeps, and the footsteps in the corridor, the gentle squeak of rubber soles on tile floor, are no more to him than footsteps in a dream, forgotten as they occur.

Fred is a nurse working on his black belt, who spends two hours after work every other night at his Kung Fu class. He says he needs more sleep during the day if he's working nights than the other way around. When he's working in the Emergency Room, he needs at least eight hours; otherwise he gets by on five or six. Dr. Will is the emergency doctor at night. At ten o'clock in the evening he has already been on duty since dawn and will work till the following dawn. Neither Fred nor Dr. Will minds working at night; in fact, they both prefer it. Fred is twenty-five, an even six feet tall: one hundred and ninety-five pounds of black assurance. Fred gets on well with nearly everyone, except for the few admissions who are so terrified of being in a hospital at all that they scream at him, or try to pick fights. When he won't fight, they call him chicken and they call him queer, and he stands with his arms folded on his chest and smiles at them.

Fred looks in on the Obstetrics ward whenever he can, on his way to Pediatrics. Through the glass he watches the row of small heads. The flesh on the soft rounded domes is as thin as eggshell; the small mouths pucker in wet asterisks. Fred and his fiancée, Lynn, have already agreed that they will have children; how many they don't know. Lynn too is a nurse, in Pediatrics. As he watches the sleeping babies, the nursery attendant on duty carefully lifts up a baby boy from his crib in the far corner of the room and shows it to Fred, smiling across the cribs in between. The infant, whose name is Rosario, moves his clenched fists against the air, somewhere between waking and sleep. Fred says he wants to have at least two children, of that he's sure. He watches the sleeping babies through the glass like a man standing on the beach watching the sea. The woman puts Rosario back in his crib after dusting his eyelids with a soft cloth. All the infants have had their eyes washed with silver nitrate at birth, to eliminate any crusting at the corners, to prevent infection. They are all silent for the moment, creating a lull in the ward.

Nurses say that babies begin to dream early. While they are still curled inside their mothers, they are experiencing that which in adults is called REM sleep. This is rapid eye movement sleep and is thought to involve constant dreaming. After birth newborn infants still spend 50 percent of their time at this level of sleep. They spend sixteen out of twenty-four hours sleeping, watching images form and disintegrate, learning associations and symbols, somehow getting to know the unknowable. They lie in their cribs with their mouths pulling open and shut, eyes following the inner display beneath lids as thin as the petals of a rose. Behind their soft foreheads, grey tissue wrinkles imperceptibly. The warm electricity of intuition charges one cell, then another. A chamber of the mind is entered, heated, and then passed by.

Across the hospital, in the rooms of the various wards, patients sleep, and cry, and pray. In Intensive Care a man holds his dying wife's hand in his; in the Emergency Room a young drug overdose victim is brought in by ambulance. A man crawls into a woman's bed in her room in the Obstetrics ward. He

is her husband and has been drinking from a bottle
of Night Train in his pocket. He insists on making
love to her. A nurse walks in, with medication for
the next day's delivery, while he is urging the woman
to raise herself up on her knees. He stops fondling
her breasts when the door opens. The wife turns her
face to the pillow, covering her open mouth to stop
the flow of hysterical laughter.

The nurse is Lois, a woman of thirty-five. In an
immediate reflex, she claps her hands together, then
turns from the room and strides out into the hallway. She sees the male nurse, sees it is Fred, and
after telling him what's going on, brings him with her
back into the room. Calmly, she tells the husband to
leave. Embarrassed, the man mumbles to himself as
he buttons his cardigan sweater around his stomach.
The male nurse asks if he needs any help getting out
the door. Lois takes the woman's pulse, mops her
brow, and stands talking softly to her for a few moments after the men have left the room.

Back at the nurses' station, Lois says these things
seldom happen. She says it is perhaps a means of reinforcement in the face of the unknown. Fred says
the husband better not come back.

The hospital night can be seen as a pale still life,
with bursts of dramatic color. The overview is of
long green and white halls, and of white shoes walking briskly to and fro. Doors open and close, and
throughout the entire hospital there is the feeling of
being plugged into an enormous machine. A sense

of pulse dominates, even in those rooms where aged bodies lie sleeping, with only the orange glow from night lamps lighting their breathing. The pulse circulates from the Intensive Care unit to the Cardiac Care ward, from the Emergency Room to the Pediatrics section, and on to Obstetrics and Gynecology.

Those who choose to work in the night do so for many reasons. In the desert hospital night the choice is exceptional: in the southern California desert the night is only a passing shadow on the sand. To those who live there, life is sustained by the day. Night is the time when one's pulse slows, and one's anxieties quicken. For the old, sleep is a sort of enemy. In the sun-baked sand that surrounds the basin and the springs, the heat of the day is always there, resting, reassuring.

In the hospitals serving the area, admissions go up after the dinner hour. Dr. Will says it is because people actually put off thinking about dealing with their aches and pains until after the sun has gone down. He says they rush in between the hours of seven and eleven each night, as if in a tribal pattern.

Dr. Will sits in the cafeteria, taking a break for a cup of coffee. He wears his green Emergency Room smock, with masks and gloves stuck in the pockets. After seventeen years in the hospital he knows pretty well how to pace himself through the night. In the space of twenty-four hours he treats between fifty and sixty-five patients in the emergency rooms: they come in with nosebleeds and pulmonary embolisms, carried in by ambulance from traffic accidents and by private car from incomplete abortions. There are wrist fractures and myocardial infarctions and flu syndromes and suicides. Everything passes through the E ward, and it is Dr. Will's business to decide what treatment is called for, and where among the various wards each patient should be sent.

Dr. Will was born in Budapest in 1904. He grew up in that city and then came to this country with his parents during the First World War. He and his brother prowled the streets of the city as boys, and he remembers finding an old print among the rubble, an old wood-block which he brought to this country but lost before he came to California. The caption was in Russian, and the translation was DEATH AND DOCTOR GOODGLASS. Dr. Will says the print is like an icon in his brain, the image of the two figures curled inward and facing each other, both in profile and caricature: an old man with a scythe faces a chubby, rather porcine doctor who holds up before him a long mirror. In it the figure of death is reflected as that of the doctor himself.

In the hallway Dr. Will stops for a moment to talk with Lois, whose work has ended for the night, and who is on her way home. She tells him about the man in his wife's bed and he smiles. After a few more words she smiles, too. The woman is now being looked after by Jean, the night nurse in labor and delivery.

A young man named Domingo comes into the life of the hospital as a code four. The state of his consciousness is unknown upon entry. The tattoo on his bare back as he stumbles against the wall is obscured by the arm of the ambulance attendant at his side. The tattoo is of a woman, smiling and smoking a cigarette. Doctor Will examines him in the first drapery cubicle of the long room, trying to establish a diagnosis. Domingo sits up repeatedly, explaining that he's taken some medication for a sprained muscle, and that maybe he took too much.

Hospital work is done in teams in the night. The people on the earlier shift say the people who work nights are a bit crazy. The people who work at night don't mind being called crazy at all.

The women who work until dawn in the hospital have children and husbands who go to school and work during the day. Fred says he and Lynn have it all worked out that as long as they both keep working nights, they'll be able to get married six months sooner, because of the difference in pay. Fred says he wouldn't mind working in Pediatrics all the time, but he thinks the Emergency Room is the most interesting part of the hospital night.

Domingo tries to get up and leave the bed where he's lying, and Fred has to restrain him. His father and two sisters come to the door of the Emergency Room and look in; then, after he quiets down, they return to the waiting room across the hall. Linda, the other nurse in the room, asks Fred if he thinks he can get a blood sample, and Fred shakes his head. He and Domingo look into each other's face, inches apart. Then Fred loosens his grip; the other man remains tense.

In the Obstetrics ward labor generally begins around 11:00 P.M. Once one woman begins labor, two or three others invariably follow. Carolyn, the charge nurse in the ward, sits on a stool next to a small desk, watching the babies through the glass. There are three areas in the ward: labor and delivery, nursery, and postpartum. There are three labor rooms and two delivery rooms. Only one of the two nurseries is used at a time, while the other is being cleaned and disinfected. Along with Carolyn, who is two months pregnant herself, there are two other women working: Jean in the nursery and Edna in the postpartum section. Jean is the oldest of the three women and moves along the nursery behind the glass, picking up the babies, checking on each, shuffling back and forth among the rows of cribs.

The three women come on at eleven, change into their nursing smocks and caps, scrub, and then move on to their separate sections. A baby born at twilight that day is the youngest in the ward; the oldest is four days old. There are seven babies altogether. One of them, Timothy, has been a premature birth and sleeps in a monitored incubator called an isolette. Babies like Timothy—called preemies by the nurses—are kept in isolation because of their vulnerability, because of the delicacy of their heartbeat. There is a bluish light in his incubator; Timothy is two days old and still is being fed intravenously, and has a slim tube down his throat as well. He has had only thirty-two weeks' gestation—forty is normal— and spent twelve days in his mother's uterus with a ruptured membrane. Timothy was delivered by Cae-

sarian section. (Carolyn says that later in life premature babies are more likely to be battered babies and
children than are babies born in the orthodox manner. It isn't easy to say why. She says that it may have
to do with their lack of contact with their mothers.)
The incubator gives off a low hum, and a light, attached to it and visible at the nurses' desk, monitors
Timothy's heart rate. The other babies in the room
jerk their heads to the right and left under their
pink and blue blankets; Jean passes among them,
pacifying those who need attention, making sure
there is no breathing blockage. Infant skin is like
litmus paper, and when breath stoppage occurs, it
changes from pink to dusky to blue to black. Even
when the babies have taken on this last hue, they can
still be brought back to normal breathing.

Carolyn, the week before, assisted at a stillbirth,
the second baby born to a mother in eight months.
The infant, like most preemies, was a breech birth,
and its lungs were too immature to support the surface tension necessary for life. Stillbirths are rare;
Caesarian sections are not all that uncommon. Four
out of the seven babies in the nursery entered their
lives this way. The hospital admits many Vietnamese
wives of American husbands who require the more
involved process of delivery. Edna says that for some
reason Philippine mothers have the fastest births of
all. The Vietnamese mothers have raw fish brought
in to feed their babies; American and Mexican
mothers from the communes around Landers and
the Noctula settlement to the north prefer vegetar-
ian beginnings and breast-feeding. Edna breast-fed

her own three children, and both she and Carolyn recommend it. They say at least half of those babies born in the hospital are breast-fed.

Mexican mothers come to the hospital from across the border in Tijuana and even Mexico City in order to have children who will be given their choice of citizenship when they reach the age of eighteen. Young people move into the area; the old who have come to the desert to retire are now joined by those who want to raise families. Ages and races mingle, in the hospital as outside. The nurses say that yellow babies are not yellow, brown babies are not brown, and black babies are not black at birth. They all come into the world a kind of off-white.

Edna says that babies become irritated when the moon is full, and that changes in tides and barometric pressure influence patterns of labor and delivery. When there are only four or five babies in the nursery, they behave more irritably than when there are thirteen or fourteen. Violent sand and wind storms outside upset some babies, while at the same time calming others. Birthrates always go down immediately before holidays.

The nightly schedule for the nurses involves weighing all the infants at one, changing their diapers, taking their temperatures, and feeding them at two. During the day they are fed every four hours; at night, after the two o'clock feeding, they are fed only if they cry for it, or if their mothers want to breast-feed them. Breast-feeding is good for the mothers as well as the babies; the infant's sucking triggers the milk and the milk triggers vaginal contractions which help the mother get back in shape. Usually, babies are given nothing to eat for from six to twelve hours after birth. At birth they are very active and agitated, and it takes from six to eight hours for them to calm down, to establish themselves in their new environment.

There is only one female G.P. working in the hospital, and all the obstetricians are male. Edna and Carolyn say that, ideally, birth should be an area of strong female reinforcement. Most mothers in labor scream for their own mothers, but no grandmothers are allowed in during delivery. The nurses say they are glad that the psychological needs of postpartum patients are now being recognized as much as the physical needs. They would, however, prefer more female obstetricians.

Four thousand babies come into the country each night, creating a small city of dreams. The nurses watch over them, as elsewhere they watch over the blinking lights of electroencephalographs. The measure of life is constant.

Doctor Goodglass leans over a female patient in the Intensive Care ward. She sees his smile through the film of her vision. Next to her bed the charge nurse, Clifford, checks the heart monitors of the other patients in the room.

Joanne, the nursing manager, says there are no rules, that people die throughout the night and throughout the day. Transitional cases slip away when they will.

When Domingo's father appears, Dr. Will tells him that his son has refused to give either a urine or a blood sample. He asks if he knows of any reason for the refusal. The father shrugs. The sisters in the waiting room look at their mother. Linda gives Domingo some ipecac syrup to drink, and then a paper cup of water. He says nothing to the nurses.

In the waiting room the doctor tells the father that Domingo took an overdose, and that it wasn't just pain-killers. The father defends his son; the sisters sit stony-faced. Domingo has been given mouth-to-mouth resuscitation in the ambulance. The two drivers stand talking to the blue-jacketed respiratory attendants. They talk about narceine.

In the Intensive Care unit of the hospital, the presence of death is always immediate. It is held off for as long as possible; ultimately, the instant of death is obliquely determined. Traces of energy from chrome machines climb through the network of liquefying cells, seldom touching sensate points. Response is nil. The old and dumb lie like aphids in their beds, bodies gripped by claws and sutures from the chrome and plexiglass machines. They do not protest their indignity, for there is no facility of communication to measure their rage. This year in California, neurological death is judged to occur when two electroencephalogram readings taken twenty-four hours apart show no discernible sign of brain activity.

An X-ray technician a few doors down from Surgery pulls out an examining table from the wall of a small room and after lying down on top of it closes her eyes for twenty minutes. She has been working for almost forty-eight hours, and the images behind her eyes are a series of exploding molecules. The black glasses she wears to read the machines have left a line across the bridge of her nose and cheeks.

At a few minutes after four, the blue light on the isolette where the infant Timothy sleeps flickers out. Jean is out of the room when the breathing stoppage occurs, and Carolyn from her desk sees the change in light out of the corner of her eye. She enters the nursery, moving directly to the isolette. She begins a series of light stroking motions against Timothy's chest and the soles of his feet, then she turns him on his side and rhythmically strokes his back. The light flickers on after ten seconds. Carolyn stands beside the crib watching the tiny movement of his chest, then, when Jean returns, resumes her station at the desk.

There is little extraneous detail in the hospital night. The instruments are functional in the extreme, plastics and gauzes and crystalline powders are passed among the nurses and orderlies without comment, without judgment. All actions prescribe to pattern. Fred moves the leads and bits of adhesive for cardiac patients from one drawer to another. There is a lull. It is nearly dawn.

At four forty-five the desert wind comes up. A man from Minnesota with a condominium apartment in town comes in talking of pain around his

kidneys. His medical history is recorded and processed immediately in a databank of gleaming steel.
Kidney stones seem the predictable diagnosis. The
wind blows through the stands of bamboo outside
the hospital; the dry stalks rub against one another,
rasping their own complaints.

At five fifteen a woman with a nosebleed comes in;
her husband waits nearby as Dr. Will packs her nose,
stopping the flow.

On the wall of the Emergency Room there are
three instruction charts. One is an identification
guide for venomous snakes, the second prescribes
procedures of immediate treatment for minor burns,
and the third is for Initial Care of the Severely
Burned Patient. The room stretches past three curtained partitions which give some privacy to each of
the patients admitted. Brown wood cabinets hang on
egg-yolk-colored walls, above beige floors, with aqua
and white curtains on ceiling tracks.

At five thirty the breast-fed babies are brought to
their mothers in their rooms in the Obstetrics ward.
The hours between five and seven are the hours of
greatest activity for the nurses; most of the mothers
have been asleep since ten the night before and
are now waking up, wanting to feed their babies.
There are five babies brought to their mothers; Timothy and another boy named David are left in the
nursery. If the mothers have elevated temperatures,
over 100 degrees, they aren't allowed to nurse. The
babies are left with the mothers for only as long as

the actual nursing takes, then they are brought back to the nursery.

Jean gives a woman her son, Rosario, and watches approvingly as she carefully brings his mouth to her breast. The pale child already has a swirl of black hair on the crown of his head; against his mother's full dark breast his small mouth and fingers open and close. His gaze wobbles upward, and his dark eyes find the eyes of his mother, seeming to rest there for a moment before they close. Rosario has entered the world without the slap that his older brothers and sisters have all endured. At twilight the day before, his head first emerged from his mother's womb, then fifteen seconds later his shoulder and arm followed. He wriggled out into life as easily as a minnow. Bulb suction was used to ease out his mouth and nose, then his shoulder. He was held head down as he emerged, so that his mother's blood would still flow into his body. He breathed his mother's oxygen for two minutes. And then the cord was cut, and tied. His parents have asked that he not be circumcised, and he hasn't been. Now he suckles at his mother's wide brown nipple as the sun comes up. The room faces east, and the first light comes into it in narrow slats through the blinds. A band of light falls across the mother's face as she looks out across the flat desert. She closes her eyes and settles into the nursing process.

The wind outside piles a thin layer of sand against the hospital wall. A pale lizard, taking its color from the day, runs the length of the building wall, then disappears.

Rosario grips his mother's skin tightly between his fingers. As the sunlight moves down from his mother's body to his own, his mouth opens around the dark nipple and he begins a gasping cry. He continues his wailing until Jean crosses to the window, pulling shut the blinds. Then he is still, and the nurse leaves the room.

Paging Joyce Camel

Las Vegas is neither town, nor city. It is a unique and specialized area unto itself, both geographically and spiritually self-sufficient, that draws its pilgrims to its center as efficiently and consistently as any medieval or Attic state. It is a desiccated Venice, a neon Andorra, an exaggeratedly unholy Holy See. Parallels with the Vatican are many, obviously drawn; like that enduring principality, Las Vegas has its cadre of devoted workers, its priests and its nuns. And it also has, as everyone knows, its very own god. Mammon like all gods appears to be aloof and indifferent to suffering. He is invisible except in his symbolic manifestations and is the focus of limitless, even obsessive, devotion. He is also, in this center in the desert that is his highest and holiest shrine, ubiquitous. In the arid night Mammon triumphs over Buddha, Allah, and Jesus Christ; his victory is facilitated nightly by all those who serve him, by those who ease the way of his pilgrims.

Those who serve are everywhere in Las Vegas;
they act as greater and lesser handmaidens to his
bidding, as the true maintainers, the upholders of
not only the faith of Mammon, but of the night itself. They stand like plastic caryatids in their casino
corners, or they roam silently, efficiently, among the
tables. These are not the ladies of the chorus, nor of
the evening; these are the women of the oasis, the
women of the Holy Mirage. It is they who are responsible for the night and its passage, they who are,
more than the men, the resort's true clergy. These
women, young and old, comprise the real sisterhood
of Mammon, the sorority of Las Vegas night.

They do not stand motionless and waiting for
long. They move about on black mesh legs, striding
back and forth each night over miles of carpet like
voluptuous spiders. They carry Keno cards, trays of
cigarettes, change for the slot machines, drinks.
They smile when they should, and when they should
is all the time. They are in positions of authority as
well as positions of glamour, but all are positions of
service. In the sandy desert they are the women of
the water jugs and millet cakes; a hundred or a thousand years ago they pursued the same rounds, in different skins, with different burdens. Now, as then,
they pass among those to whom they are largely invisible. The travelers who order drinks and cigarettes and cheese omelettes do so with only the
mind's left hand; the right hand is perpetually busy
with the real business and purpose of their stay, the
spending of self, the casting of ego upon baize waters, the gambling.

The travelers come at night, checking into the hotel at its main desk, a long bank of counters overlooking the vast casino and its rows and rows of slot machines, blackjack tables, crap tables, and roulette wheels.

Marie, the night clerk, welcomes them, giving them their room keys, arranging for their luggage to be carried up, explaining what little there is to explain about check-out times and other regulations and schedules. As often as not, the arriving guests send their baggage up with the bellman and move directly down into the churning sea of chips and dealers and whirring machines. Until they have made their first pass with the dice, stuffed their first quarter into a slot machine, they are not yet where they want to be, they have not yet presented themselves at the shrine.

Downtown, in the older section of Las Vegas, away from the Strip, in one of the casinos a glowing golden horseshoe eight feet tall arches over and around a sheet of plexiglass. Pressed inside the sheet are five rows of twenty $10,000 bills. There is a young photographer named Nancy who will take your photograph for free, standing in front of the million-dollar sheet, beneath the horseshoe's arch. Nancy wants to become a dealer but for the time being is happy enough working with her camera and her customers. She doesn't tell her subjects to say *cheese,* she tells them instead to say *million,* or *money.* She gets a lot of cowboys, and when they come in, the word she asks for is *whiskey.* From time to time she tells them to say whichever word they prefer:

money or *sex*. When she first began working as the horseshoe photographer, she was afraid that she'd never get used to the noise of the casino around her. There was one day when she went totally deaf for an hour; after that one hour, when her sense of hearing did return, she was somehow able to get used to the sound of the ringing slot machines and the crush of voices. It was in that same first week of work that she encountered the woman who asked to be photographed kneeling before the horseshoe in an attitude of prayer. The woman was middle-aged and well dressed; she knelt on a silk scarf on the carpeted floor.

People who ask to be photographed kissing the plexiglass sheet are not uncommon. A man from Ohio kissed it twenty-three times and asked that his picture be taken during the twenty-fourth kiss.

Marie estimates the number of people she has checked in during the six years she has worked there at well over ten thousand. She prefers working at night, coming on at midnight and working till eight in the morning. Her husband works the same hours; his working night is as busy as his wife's.

Marie is explaining to a Mr. Moore that unfortunately she has no record of his reservation. He stands before the counter, deeply tanned, in a blood-colored shirt, frowning through his tan, seemingly on the edge of anger.

"Would there have been a different spelling on that name? Would someone else have made the reservation in their name, Mr. Moore?" Marie is solicitous, looking first at the man and then at his companion, a silent, attractive woman in her twenties. Mr. Moore is perhaps fifty-five.

"No other spelling, no other name," he tells her, gruffly. "I made the reservation last week and checked on it myself this morning from L.A."

Marie turns and is checking alternate spellings when Mr. Moore abruptly pivots and walks away from the desk and back out into the night. Neither he nor his companion has any luggage. They are replaced at the counter by two men from Switzerland, who hand their red passports across to her and stand gazing out at the tables while she checks them in. She asks if they need help with their bags, and they say they think not. Each has two bags, rather heavy, and after they've been given their keys, they carry their luggage to the elevators unaided. Europeans almost always carry their own bags, while Americans seldom do, even if it's a matter of a flight bag and a single valise. Attaché cases are kept firmly in hand by all.

Down in the pit, in the casino itself, the dealers are taking their twenty-minute break. They walk off the floor in groups and pairs, slowly, in no particular hurry, relaxing. Behind the tables the men who replace them look invulnerable; under spotlights shining down from between beaded chandeliers, their hands on the green tables seem enormous, the fingers and wrists pinpointed by the light, made more capable, more authoritative, more adept. The cards that are dealt by these hands, beneath these shoulders, seem by comparison insignificant. The faces of the dealers are dark masks—the question

they hear over and over again each night is, Why
don't you smile? Dealers invite no confidences and
give no advice. Dealers are serious, priestly, intent.

In the big casinos there are women dealers as well
as men, but they are still the overall exception. Black
hands or white hands, they are masculine hands
flipping over the cards, masculine hands spinning
the roulette wheels. The idea of a female supervising
the dice tables has never been entertained. In the
dealers' lounge the men sit among themselves, smoking, talking, at ease. They play hearts during their
break, or pitch. They don't drink coffee because it
makes them sweat. They return to their tables when
the twenty minutes have passed and the next group
goes off. A floorman acts as the nucleus for each
group of four tables, standing in the center of the
four corners of their square, supervising, overseeing
payoffs. It seems a grim business amid the lights and
the milling players; no matter how light the gestures
of turning the cards or the wheel, the profession is a
serious one; the odds, all odds, are heavy.

The women move among the tables and about the
room, slowly or briskly, revolving, turning, then revolving once again.

Anna is a striking young woman with soft ash-
blonde hair and green eyes. Her face is fine-boned
and classic; she gives the impression in repose of
knowing how to spend money, and of having spent a
great deal. She is tall and slim and has worked as a
cigarette girl in the casinos of Las Vegas for nearly
eight years. Her job gives her more freedom than
the other women; she is a self-contained unit with her

tray of different brands, and as a franchisee she is
responsible to herself rather than to the various restaurants or casino bars. She can, therefore, walk
away from anyone who starts to hassle her. Her husband works in another casino. Most casinos prohibit
husbands and wives' working together, and so there
is a lot of mixing between other women's husbands
and other men's wives. It is in many ways a town
designed for the divorce courts; marriages that take
place at the Chapel of the Roses or the Wee Kirk o'
the Heather chapels on Las Vegas Boulevard often
make it to the Getaway Motel nearby, and not much
further. Anna has seen Vegas marriages come and
go and is more than a little proud of her own, of its
success. There are no children.

The cigarette girl outfit she wears while working is
of her own design; she and the other girl she works
with have had to pay for them, but they don't mind
the expense. The black formal jacket over ruffled
shirt and the black silk tie give the job style. Anna's
attitude is that if she's got to work in Las Vegas, she's
got the job that's best for her. She is thirty-one and a
realist.

Over the loudspeaker comes a woman's voice re-
peating the words *Paging Joyce Camel.* Among the
other names periodically paged, the name passes
without notice; it is a noise, which like all casino
noises is soon absorbed into the rug. It is a call for
cigarettes, and Anna strides to a gold house telephone to answer it. She is told by the operator that a
man needs Dunhills in the casino restaurant, and she
leaves the well of tables, crosses the lobby, and de-
livers the pack to the customer. Whether it is Anna

or Gladys, the girl she alternates with, the call is the same. When the cigarettes are delivered or when a customer comes up to them on the floor, the girls always announce the dollar price before handing over the pack. Most of the time customers pay without complaint; some of the time they do not pay, and the trip to the bar or coffee shop is made for nothing. When the customer decides not to buy, it is usually when his wife is at his elbow saying a dollar is too much when they can get them in a machine, if only they could find one, for sixty-five cents. There is seldom a tip on the dollar, no matter who is buying.

Night in the casinos seems a more natural state than day. The focus of gambling activity appears more normal with a black backdrop; Phoebus and Mammon are in this way contradictory. When the desert sun is shining outdoors, indoors in the casino it is always night, always separated from outdoor rhythms, outdoor elements.

Even the restaurants on either side of the casino pit serve up their food in the manner of night fare rather than day fare. There is a bit of garnish with every course, a sprig of parsley and a single radish beside a plate of bacon and eggs. The waitresses are dressed in yellow, but it is closer to the color of gold than the color of sunshine.

On the walls of the restaurants, instead of damp-eyed children, or seascapes lathered up with palette knives, there hang framed Keno boards. The $25,000 figures are bright pink against the black, the numbers beneath lighting up the winning sequences in their ten columns. The customers in the restaurant at their stools and tables glance up now and again to check the numbers on these boards with the look of travelers peering through a window, checking on the weather.

Anna, after giving her customer his pack of Dunhills, stops at the cash register to talk to Sarah, the night cashier.

"What are we reading tonight?" she wants to know, and reaches down and under the counter in front of Sarah to find out. She brings out a paperback copy of *Wuthering Heights* and holding it out before her gives Sarah a long look of amazement.

"I thought I'd read it again," Sarah says, taking it from her. Her tone is apologetic.

"I don't know where you get your books, honey. I really don't. Why don't you read something a little hotter, a little more with it. I mean, this is kid stuff."

"It is not," Sarah replies, replacing it on the shelf.

A customer comes up and gives Sarah his check, signing it with his room number. She takes it from him and gives him a smiling Thank you. Anna rests her tray on the counter after he has gone.

"Are you going out after work?" she asks, in the manner of one who has asked the question countless times, and who knows what the answer will be.

"Not today . . . I have to do some shopping; I have to pick up some things for the weekend." Sarah's dark eyes remain fixed on her book as she answers.

"My cousin Harry is here from Chicago for a few days, and I thought maybe I'd set you two up. He's kind of fun. You'd like him."

Sarah makes no reply, and after a moment Anna says, "If you change your mind, let me know."

She walks off, adjusting the straps of her tray, heading back down into the casino. Sarah sits quietly on her cashier's stool, waiting for checks. She smooths out the pile she has already amassed and, opening the cash drawer, rearranges the rolls of quarters and dimes in the back tray. Satisfied that all is in order, she carefully recloses it and folds her hands in her lap. She sits quietly, from time to time smoothing out the creases of her gold uniform dress, patting her long dark hair into place.

From her seat she can look out into the lobby, to the gift shop across the lobby from the main desk, to the other gift shop in the arcade, now closed for the night. At the end of the arcade, just before the bank of elevators, someone has forgotten to turn off the revolving barber pole in front of the Unisex barbershop and beauty parlor. It turns slowly, its stripes coiling silently upward; the stripes, rather than the classic red, white, and blue of barbershops everywhere else in the world, are three different shades of money-green.

The high rollers come out after midnight. At three thirty or four the ring of players around the tables of the casino has thinned; fewer bodies press against the wood and baize. It is at this time of night that men with their own retinues, and their own brand of credit, appear in the casino.

There are familiar and unfamiliar faces among them, and the bar girls and cigarette girls and waitresses know, if they have been at their work long

enough, which of the customers will appreciate a
Havana cigar and which a bullshot or dry vermouth.
A lot of the dealers prefer working the tables at this
hour. The mood is aggressively no-nonsense, for the
men who play are playing for high stakes. A man
walks away from the dice table having made $10,000
in a little more than forty minutes. Another moves
away from the blackjack tables, down twice that
amount after an hour and a half. Tokes, those por-
tions of the winnings that are left for the player's
dealer at the end of his play, are correspondingly as
high as the stakes. The casino is quieter at this hour;
the performers at the clubs and show rooms in the
different hotels have given their last rendition of
"My Way" and "The Impossible Dream," the come-
dians have sent their last insult wrapped in humor
and sweat flying out over the footlights. Their audi-
ences have since swarmed out of the show rooms,
back to the casinos, to wander in a disquieted herd
past the late players, reluctantly moving toward their
hotel bedrooms. The men have one last throw of the
dice, the women feed the slot machines one last
quarter, before settling down to a few hours' sleep.
This last play is done as a gesture to the deity, perhaps—a votive prayer before retiring. The high rollers pay the tourists no more attention than a domi-
nant male in a tribe of baboons pays the roistering
adolescent males. Unless they in some way threaten,
they do not exist.

The roulette ball is sent spinning around the
wheel, its speed decelerating with each revolution,
slowing, held by the focus of so many eyes in a kind
of stop-motion, willed to stop at each player's square,

its speed waning harshly, randomly. It bounces, bounces again, and comes to rest on number thirty-six, black. A heavyset man in sunglasses mumbles to his companion, his companion mumbles to the dealer, and the pile of red chips is divided, placed on black and even. The ball is again sent revolving; it spins around the wheel twenty-one times, stopping on black, on an even number, once more.

The face of the player is immobile. Though his winnings in two revolutions have amounted to four figures, he slides his heavy body off the stool and moves impassively away, his pleasure in winning buried deep, uncommunicated, uncommunicable. The joy of winning at high stakes is not the obvious rush of emotion, the quick release, that one hundred quarters tumbling out of a slot machine produces. It is a reinforcement of self, of personal order. The big winner high roller moves from table to table in a condition not unlike a state of grace; until he falls from grace his movements are blessed, his winnings assured. This condition is in its way casino alpha. It is not available every night in the casino; the majority of evenings and mornings provide the player with approximations: small triumphs, rituals without substance. The chips are merely wafers most of the time, and true communion is elsewhere, at other tables, in other gaming rooms. Still, the tokens of worship are useful; they maintain the connection just as bread and wine maintain theirs. These plastic tokens, too, are symbols of faith; tokens of gratitude, tokens of thanks and redemption. And a token is also a toke, a small slice of the winner's pie, a taste of his bread, a mini-relic.

The high roller moves on, the twin pieties of grace
and luck dancing behind his black-shaded eyes.

Anna's husband says a winning streak is, simply,
going too far. It's not pulling back when reason says
you should. The impulse is to hang onto the streak
as if it were an enormous marlin at the end of a line.

After 4:00 A.M. the slot floormen bring in the
nickels and quarters. The rolls of coins are carried in
on three large wagons, like circus wagons, and rolled
the length of the casino to the large safe to be stored.
These are the coins from the slot machines; nickels
packed tightly in blue wrappers, quarters in orange.
The slot floormen are at either end of the wagons,
pushing and pulling slowly, pale heavy men in
shirtsleeves.

They greet the girls as they pass with a solemn
nod or even a smile. For Anna there is a solemn nod.

For Sally there is a smile.

Sally is a cocktail waitress. She wore earth shoes
with her waitress outfit for three months before anyone noticed and asked her to change them. Now she
wears black wedgies, more in harmony with her red
velvet and black taffeta uniform. She is not so fortunate as Anna and has had no say in the design of the
short dress she wears. All the bar girls wear the same
short dress and black mesh stockings. Only the shoes
vary from feet to feet. Walking across the miles of
carpet she crosses each night, her shoes are important to her, and when she buys them she selects them

with care, going so far as to measure the lift of the
arch and heel. Anything with more than an inch and
a half elevation throws her body too far forward and
puts knots in her calf muscles and, over a period of
weeks, in the small of her back.

Sally stands watching the row of dice tables, a slim
girl with black bangs. She appears to be barely out of
high school, and her makeup, or lack of it, empha-
sizes the look and makes her presence in the red and
black outfit improbable and therefore rather
naughty. Alert, she waits for the signal—the clap of
hands, or the table light switched on—that the floorman uses to summon her to the side of the players
who might want a complimentary drink. The clap
comes and she moves quickly to the end of the table
where two black men in silk shirts are playing. The
first man orders a Dewars and soda, the second a gin
and tonic. Their wives are with them and each asks
for a pepper vodka. Sally writes the orders on her
pad, then takes it directly to the large central bar
where the other girls from the slot machine section
are waiting for their orders. All three waitresses get
their drinks in short order, and Sally is back at the
table before the man with the dice has completed his
last pass. She is handing the vodkas to the two
women when he rolls his second eight and lets out a
whoop of exultation. The two women hug the man,
his companion slaps first his palm, then his back.
Sally waits for a moment, but only a moment, after
she's handed them all their glasses, before turning to
move off to the next table to pick up the empty
glasses there.

"Sweetheart, wait a minute," the gambling man

calls after her. "If you think I'm going to stiff somebody who's just brought me this good luck drink,
forget it!"

He takes two five-dollar chips from the stack in his
hand and gives them to her. "Don't wander too far
away, okay?"

She assures him she won't, that she'll be only a few
feet away if he needs her. She picks up two empty
glasses from the next table, takes them to the bar,
then recrosses the room and returns to her spot a
short distance away from the cashier's cage.

It's always either good luck or bad luck. There is
no such thing as medium luck. A lot of the drinks
she brings to the table are good luck bourbons and
good luck gins, but a lot of them turn out very
quickly to be bad luck whiskey sours. Sally doesn't
think she is lucky, she thinks she is basically unlucky
and doesn't do much gambling as a result. Her husband gets upset with her when she shoots craps, because she always seems to forget and bets both Come
and Field.

Sally is not without her discontents. She spent a
year in the East, and was trained there as a fashion
designer. She painted, then, and designed both
men's and women's clothes, and thought she'd even-
tually settle in New York, in the large world of fashion and design. Instead, after a year she came back
to Nevada to work in the casinos for a little while, to
make enough money to finance her big push in the
East. And then she met her husband, and they were
married in one of the local wedding chapels, the
kind with marquees that advertise on Las Vegas
Boulevard:

THREE SELECTIVE WEDDINGS
CALIFORNIA CHECKS OKAY
FLOWERS 24 HOURS

Both she and her husband assumed their friends
would give them some sort of wedding reception,
but none of them did. Husband and wife then settled into a routine, each working in the casino, just
for a while, because the money was good and the actual labor not that difficult. The just for a while has
now been five years.

The routine for Sally is sleeping till one or one
thirty in the morning, then getting up to start them
both on their way. She finds that she's seldom
hungry at that hour; she eats a bit of stuffing left
over from a girl friend's birthday turkey, maybe a
glass of milk, depending on how her stomach feels,
and sometimes, but not always, a cup of coffee. If
she has one cup she has two. She also puts something out for Moonshine, the puppy they've recently
acquired. It takes ten minutes to drive from the Valley in to the casino; her husband, Joe, leaves an hour
later than she, to make his four to noon shift. She
starts at two thirty. The casino night shifts cut into
each other at irregular hours. Some women begin at
six, some at eleven, and others, like Sally, between
two and three in the morning. Joe and Sally's house
is small by Las Vegas standards but has two bedrooms, one of which Joe now uses to store his photo-
graphic equipment. There is a yard where Moonshine spends the better part of his life. Sally isn't
much for gardening, especially not since the day she

encountered a rattlesnake where she had thought to put in a bed of marigolds.

Her fair skin makes sunbathing nearly impossible in the desert, yet she and Joe like to play tennis and frequently do after leaving work each morning. They find they spend their most agreeable time together in the hours after work, before they go to bed at five or six. The air conditioner in their bedroom screens out neighborhood noise and neither of them has much trouble falling asleep. Sometimes, either after work or before bed, they'll have a joint of marijuana. It doesn't keep Joe from sleeping, but it does Sally; she wishes it would simply relax her. She gets by on six hours of sleep, whereas Joe requires at least eight. It's all a matter of metabolism, Sally says, and Joe more or less agrees.

Marie at the desk is talking with Agnes, one of the clerks at the all-night souvenir shop that operates next to the casino restaurant. Agnes is a grandmother, a woman in her late fifties with grey-blonde hair teased into a brittle helmet around her lined, carefully made-up face.

"Well, I've been here five years, and it's never happened before, so far as I know. It makes me shiver, I can tell you." Agnes keeps a bespectacled eye on her counter across the lobby as she talks, making sure her relief girl isn't letting any sales go by. She also watches as two security police, women in dresses similar to her own, systematically sift through the shop's drawers and showcases. They appear to be taking inventory.

Marie answers her calmly, "It's only Mafia threats, Agnes. It's one family letting another know they're around, that's all. There's no bomb here, just you wait and see. It's Mafia P.R., that's all it is, and I'm not worried about it one bit."

Agnes's face wrinkles, unconvinced. The security women finish one line of showcases and move on to the next. Behind her desk Marie moves about briskly. In Marie's life there is an emphasis on order and economy; she believes in the power of positive action and is able to ignore what she considers to be negative details. The bomb threat, telephoned in to the casino an hour before, is, so far, just such a negative detail.

Agnes returns to her counter, grim-faced. The two policewomen look up and nod at her reassuringly. It is difficult to imagine a bomb going off in these surroundings; a boy of fourteen is standing at the magazine rack reading an article on fruit bats in a copy of *Field and Stream* while his mother inspects a rack of turquoise jewelry; a tall, thin, grey-haired man in a beige leisure suit brings a dozen postcards to the counter, pays for them, and asks if there is a stamp machine nearby. It all seems calm, with people moving about in a predictable and comfortable rhythm. Marie is probably right; a bomb scare is irrelevant.

Except that while Agnes is busy lulling herself back into a sense of security, above her in the tenth-floor lobby of the hotel an undercover policewoman named Linda is placing a manila envelope with $22,000 inside it on top of a Coca-Cola machine. The phoned-in threat has stipulated that a cashier should bring the money first to the eighth floor by one elevator and transfer to the tenth by another and place it on the machine in the lobby. Linda, in her knit suit, makes a convincing cashier; she is new on the security force and so far her only dangerous encounter has been with an Argentine drunk in the ladies' room. After delivering the envelope, she steps back into the elevator, relieved that no one has been waiting by the machine, and presses the button for the ground floor, the casino floor.

Downstairs in the casino other security men and women are moving through the thicket of tables and slot machines slowly, invisibly. Linda hurries to the security desk at the rear of the casino, where two men in blue uniforms and another in plainclothes are listening in on the line to a tenth-floor room that has been staked out. The plainclothesman, Tom, is working as Linda's partner. It is only a matter of minutes until a young man dressed in a white uniform appears to pick up the envelope; he is surrounded immediately by the police and FBI agents as he moves from the Coke machine to the elevator. He tells the arresting officers that he works in the hotel kitchen, and that while on his break he has been approached by a grey-haired man in the casino who has promised him fifty dollars to pick up the envelope for him.

Hearing this, Linda and Tom leave the security desk and move to the lobby in front of the elevators, where they stand talking in the guise of tourists.

The kitchen worker is instructed by the men on the tenth floor to take the money envelope back down to the casino and find and deliver it to the man who hired him. Shaken by his involvement in the extortion, he is willing to do what they ask; he walks out of the elevator on the main floor a few minutes after Tom and Linda have taken up their station, clutching the envelope as if it were the bomb itself. Before crossing into the casino section, he looks into the gift shop and there sees the grey-haired man at the counter. Forgetting his instructions, he looks around for someone to alert; the grey-haired man sees his look of panic and, instead of walking toward him, turns and walks briskly toward the other end of the shop. As he reaches the magazine stand, the two women who have been searching the shop, alerted by their walkie-talkies, move directly into his path and, one on either side, take him firmly into custody. His face is a rigid mask of calm. They each hold him by the arm as if he is a favorite uncle or an old friend, talking to him good-naturedly as they escort him away. Fifteen minutes later the news is quickly relayed to all security personnel that the bomb has been found taped to the entrance arch over the main door of the empty casino show room. It is dismantled quickly by the bomb squad, a young man from Utah, who announces that because of faulty wiring, it would never have gone off at all.

Agnes smooths down the hair on the crown of her head with one hand while with the other she straightens the display of postcards the grey-haired customer has left strewn on the counter. She checks her appearance in the jewelry counter mirror, then looks around to make sure the two security women who have gone through her shelves have put everything back in order. She remarks to herself that it is strange for them to have gone off that way with the grey-haired customer; perhaps he too is an undercover policeman; perhaps they've all been called away to check on the bomb somewhere else.

From across the carpeted lobby Marie watches Agnes as she mumbles to herself, as she tries to make sense out of what has happened. Suddenly, it all fits into place, and Agnes's troubled expression changes to one resembling that of a deer surprised by headlights on the highway. Marie looks away, before Agnes's eyes catch her own, and with an amused smile opens a file of upcoming reservations for a Two Guys chain store convention the following week.

Sarah in the restaurant needs a lot of time to get herself going. She worked the swing shift from four to midnight for a year, then switched over to graveyard three years ago and now wouldn't go back to days. Her work as cashier is not nearly so demanding at night as it would be during the day; the customers who present their bills for bacon and bleu cheese salad, or cherry cheesecake, usually sign for them with their room numbers, so she isn't even required to make change very often. When there is little business, after four thirty or so in the morning, she is able to read as she sits on her high-backed stool behind the counter.

There are those who choose the night, and those who have the night thrust upon them. Sarah is one of those who has chosen. She lives now by herself, a woman of thirty-two, with dark shoe-button eyes and long dark hair. She looks more Spanish or Mexican than English-Irish, which is what she is. She is a short woman with a good figure; sitting quietly on her stool she seems composed and self-reliant, attractive. When she first came to Las Vegas four years ago, she had a flashier look about her; her lids were coated a silver green and she used quite a lot of eyeliner. Now the look is quieter, subtler.

The night cradles some and disrupts others; Sarah has found that she has more time at night, and that the time she has is more soothing to her. She was born in Phoenix, born in the sunshine, and moved to California soon after high school. She married a man who played electric guitar; there were two children born in her mid-twenties. Both of them now live with her husband's parents in Orange County; she is divorced from her husband and would prefer never to see him again. She has very little to say about her past, about her life in that period, as if it now belonged to someone else. It was during her time in California, immediately after her divorce and before she moved to Las Vegas, that Sarah developed the trick of drawing out the small processes of life, such as drying her hair or washing the dishes, until the rituals of order became long and satisfying processes of discipline and restraint. She would move about the small kitchen of her apartment for hours, preparing, eating, and then cleaning up after a not very elaborate meal.

When she arrived in Las Vegas she worked first as

a Keno girl, running back and forth from the Keno chairs to the bar with the blacked-in cards, then as a cocktail waitress. Neither job fit her pace. In the casino restaurant she began as a waitress, but after she'd sat on the cashier's stool, she decided that she was happiest there. She was able to make change efficiently; she was able to remember how many quarters and how many nickels were in each compartment. She sometimes pulled out the change without looking, to show herself, and the world, she could do it.

She found when she started working nights that the day had never really interested her that much.

She arises as far after noon as is possible. If it is two o'clock and she still thinks a minute or two more would be good for her, then she stays in bed. Taking her time, and doing a good job, have become very important to her.

Sarah lives not far from Anna, in an apartment house called Desert Estates. There is a large glass door that opens to a small patio where two potted yucca sit, impervious to the wind and the sun during the day. Sarah sleeps with a dark maroon drapery drawn across the window, against the light.

Sarah has chosen the Las Vegas night because it gives her something the day has never been able to provide her with: a sense of security through order, and a sense of calm. In the casino night there are more spaces between things—between tables, between players and customers, between conversations—and yet there is still the appearance of a great deal of excitement and activity.

From her cashier's perch she can see the dealers,

the bar girls, the gambling men, the tired children, the exhausted wives. They all pass before her, close enough to touch, but she has no real involvement with them, needs no involvement other than the systematic tabulation of how much they have put in their stomachs, and of how many nickels and quarters and silver dollars it has cost.

It is the appearance of activity that satisfies Sarah, the feeling of being involved in life and yet being safely apart from it. Her smile and her Thank you are not so much directed at each customer as at the circumstances of night that permit her such simple relationships. The essence of Las Vegas night, casino night, is that it is all, after everything else, so mechanical.

An old woman in soiled black pedal pushers and Mexican sandals roams through the maze of slot machines, a cup of quarters in one hand, a cup of gin in the other. A middle-aged man in a Stetson and a Nudie cowboy shirt, having obviously drunk too much, bolts from the dice table and stops, doubling over to his knees near the entrance to the deserted show room. He seeks no living hands to support him; instead he hangs onto a seven-foot stand-up photo mannequin of the show room's blonde singing star. Smiling its sugary smile, it bobs back and forth as he shakes. He regains his feet and stands with his hands on its shoulders, leaning against it.

There are in Las Vegas moments when one feels on a different planet entirely, or more precisely, on a totally mechanized space station where the process of emotional give and take is simply an anachronism. Everything is coded, everything is shorthand. The

movement of the roulette ball is the movement of
Anna and Sally circling among the tables; the matching of hotel guest with hotel room is the matching of
cherries and oranges on the slots. Ultimately, the
women serve as just so many glittering cogs in the
enormous machine. Ultimately, they and the machine are one.

Out in the desert the night blinks and it is day.
The casino unplugs certain of its fuses; the women,
released, drift away. They leave as the sun is coming
up. Outside, on the greens and tees of the golf
course adjoining the casino, the sprinkler systems
come on. The first shafts of sunlight shoot down
over the grass from the silhouette of jagged mountains against the sky; the greyness of the sky takes on
the first grains of color.

Anna stays in the casino longer than usual, linger-
ing over a cup of coffee in the restaurant with her
cousin Harry. Linda changes from her on-duty suit
to a pair of off-duty slacks, eager to get home to tell
her mother and sister all about the night's bomb
scare. She is too keyed-up to sleep.

Sally sits in her car in the parking lot, waiting for
Joe, for the two of them to have breakfast at a Pan-
cake House off the Strip. It is her first real meal of
the day, and she is hungry.

Agnes leaves a few minutes early. This is a Monday, and her son, who works as a bar boy, is coming
over to spend the late afternoon and evening with
her, on his night off. She drives to a 7-11 near the
casino that is open twenty-four hours to buy more
potatoes for that night's meal.

Marie is asleep by nine o'clock; lately she has taken

to swallowing half a yellow valium before getting into bed. She says it is because her husband comes home at different times, and she doesn't like to be awakened once she has fallen asleep. When he does come in, she doesn't open her eyes but only turns slightly in her sleep.

Sarah sits in her half-lit room, combing out her long hair.

Still Water

Night on the water is an element in itself. Along
the salt marshlands and estuaries of the South Carolina coast, the feeling of stillness in the night is totally compelling: small sounds of life impressed
against this stillness do not register on the ear or
mind until after they have passed. A frog chirps in a
freshwater pond, a low flying gull calls to another
across the mud flats, the gentle neighing of a night-
grazing pony rises up and disappears into the darkness. Only the afterimages remain. It is as if all
sounds are echoes of themselves, even at the moment in which they occur.

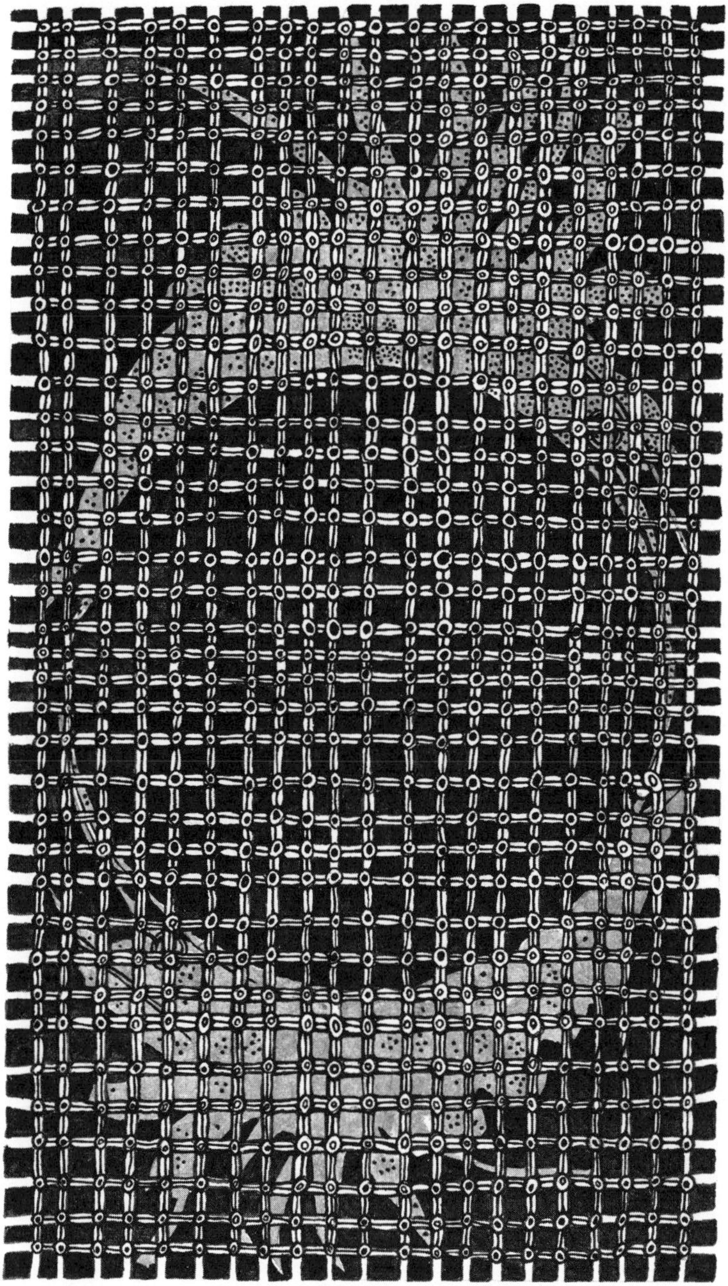

Here, the movement of the tide is the measure of
the night. There is a twelve-hour swing from high
tide to low tide and back again; as the earth and
moon pull apart, the salty water of the marshes eases
out to open sea and back, dropping a distance of between six and eight feet. The shoreline erodes, a
few inches, a few years, and then an unexpected current flows through the low islands and piles up new
patterns of sand and mud, of marsh grass and sea
grape, along the shore. The sea life follows the tides,
and the milling young of shad and trout, crab and
shrimp, move along with the current, dependent on
it for food and warmth and life.

The surface of the brown water is broken by mullet feeding in the shallows, diving upward and
breaking into the cool night air, swimming through
it for only a few seconds, then splashing backward. A
night heron stalks small fish and insects across the
flats, dipping its elegant head to the water, its beak
to the mud.

Somewhere, a mare whinnies at her foal. The
larger part of the stock on the farms and plantations
along the Inland Waterway is asleep at night. On
Wadmalaw Island, south of the Bay of Charleston, a
herd of Brahman cattle lie unmoving in the grass beneath a grove of magnolia and pine trees. Across the
dirt road from the cattle, a half-dozen ranch horses
stand drowsing near the water's edge. A blue-eyed
roan casts his gaze out across the water to where the
mullet jump, and beyond, to where a blinking channel marker lights a shoal on the far side of the
Sound. Wadmalaw Island, named after a small Indian tribe of the region, is an irregular triangle of

sand and soil some twelve miles long and five miles wide. Wadmalaw River is fed by Stono River and Church Creek from the northeast; at the southwestern edge it picks up the water of Toogoodoo Creek as well. At high tide the island is bounded by water on all sides. From the landing at New Cut Plantation one can look north past Goshen Point and the Church Flats to the soft glow of the city of Charleston in the northeastern distance. It is an ancient island, nibbled at by the Atlantic for more centuries than are remembered, with the pace of its farming and fishing moving along at time-worn rhythms.

The night sea maintains life, holds it in a state of floating suspension. From the landing at New Cut, the view is a landscape of waiting, where life hangs suspended beneath the stars. The passage of time has no measure other than the tides and sky. The night marks itself with stars; fixed, even as they shift their patterns, after a second or an hour they are suddenly changed. The Summer Triangle has slid into oblivion, the handle of the Dipper is buried beneath the horizon, and the Pleiades have crossed without seeming to from the east to the western sky. Time and the planets pass unheeding; they are not seen to move and yet each night they pass over seas and continents. And each night they are still and remain: glowing moments sustained, moments without movement.

John Mack is a river fisherman at night, a man who has spent the better part of his life fishing off Wadmalaw. He was born on the island, just as his parents were born on it before him. He and his wife have over the years sent all their children through college, from their oldest son, Jesse, down to their youngest set of twins, Martha and John, now nineteen. The children have grown up and traveled away from the island, working at jobs in other cities and towns, as far north as New York City. Some of them have come back home, and now there are nine grandchildren as well. All the men in John's family have grown up fishing, just as John grew up being shown by his own father where and when the sea bass would gather, where the shrimp would tend to be thickest in the shallows.

In the summer dog days, with the day heat gathering on the island, thick and heavy as the brown water of the Sound, John regularly goes out netting for shrimp at night. In July the soft mud of the rivers and creeks around Wadmalaw keeps the water murky. Later in the year, when the mud hardens and the water clears, he goes out gigging—spearfishing from the boat for the larger trout and shad and bass that pass through the Sound. Fish are ample in the waters around the island; John tells of going out three years ago on Christmas Eve, fishing through the night and coming in with the big fish piled slithering to the gunwales of his boat. The fish, sold in Charleston to a wholesaler rather than directly at market, had to be brought into town by truck rather than in the trunk of his battered white Plymouth Belvedere sedan; the haul was 550 pounds of speckled trout and bass. It is a haul John is justly proud of. October, November, December: these are the months in which he most enjoys the activity of fishing, the challenge of the larger fish. These are the months when the nights are cool, and a man standing in the bow of his boat can see out over the lantern, down into the clear water. Then, the big fish mill about and feed, curious about the light, ready to be gigged, at a distance of six or nine feet out from the boat.

The boat is twelve feet long and painted grey. Now, in the heat of July, it contains two cans for bailing, a screen at the center to keep the incoming shrimp from swimming or floating into the stern, a makeshift gasoline lantern shield at the bow, and a pole. John brings with him each night a seven-and-a-half-horsepower outboard motor; by day the boat is kept tied to the dock of New Cut Plantation, rising and lowering with the movement of the day tides. He comes down to the water each night at half-tide, in late summer between 10:00 P.M. and 2:00 A.M.

The process of shrimping seems a deceptively simple one. John and his son, after moving their gear from the car into the boat, untie the boat and cast off gently from the dock. The dock is framed by darkness; across the broad expanse of lawn that slopes down to the reeds and barnacles of the bank, the only movement comes from beetles and fireflies. Tent caterpillars hang in gauze clumps from trees along the road; at the landing, leeches and slugs cling to the oily wooden pilings. John and his son slowly pole out of the mud next to the dock; as the long boat skims slowly over the water's surface, John, Sr., sits in the bow, with John, Jr., poling from the stern. The boat drifts away from the dock,

moving eastward along the coast of the island. After
nearly five decades on these waters, John feels its
movement and the ebb and flow of the tide without
having to think about it. His day spent overseeing
the corn and cattle, the horses and the pigs, maintaining the life of New Cut Plantation, may be his
second nature by now, but this is his first. His face is
broad and his movements calm, and he moves with
quiet control. He began fishing at an early age, like
other children of the Waterway, first going out with
his own father late in the season, a good-looking,
eager young boy in the 1920s, learning to fish for
the big mullet, trout, and sea bass. He says now that
no matter what happens, no matter how long he
stays around, he'll always do his night shrimping.
Being on the water at night seems natural and necessary; he loves the sense of floating freedom, of drifting slowly as he will where he will, alone, or with his
son at the rudder. His sense of ease on the water is
not merely the ease one feels at being in one's own
domain—it comes as much from knowing that whoever partakes of the water and the fish at night is
welcome to both; that the fish belong to anyone and
everyone. The sense of bounty is nearly biblical. No
fishing rights limit the water, in a country where
zoning rights still limit the land.

The men move along the muddy shore, the boat
passing quietly past a large freshwater pond where a
lone ancient alligator lies among lily pads, and where
peeper frogs cry out in long six-syllable stanzas. The
full white lilies bend on their fleshy stalks; the rippling movement of a water snake makes the broad

green pads bob and edge slightly apart. A frog comments; a black bird in its nest opens, then silently closes, its beak.

John stands in the bow and casts out his net. The net is a mesh of white nylon, gathered and lead-weighted lightly around its noose. (Nylon lasts four or five years, whereas cotton lasts only one season.) John pitches the net out and, directly it hits the water, pulls its circle taut, trapping the shrimp. In an extension of the same motion, he pulls net and shrimp together back into the boat. With each throw the movement is the same: a slight looping through the air, followed by the soft impact of nylon on water. John secures the net's end between his teeth as he sends it out, while with his powerful arm he casts the loop over the milling shrimp.

As the boat passes, the shrimp leap up out of the brown water, hurling themselves a foot or more above its surface. The net closes around them and they are immediately pulled into the boat and emptied into the hold; their heads light up with a bluish-white alarm signal as they are first aroused, then trapped in the net. In the wash behind the boat, their incandescent heads are like swirls of fallen stars; the boat moves on and through them as they rise upward in jerking spasms, after it passes burrowing downward again in the soft mud.

Ahead of the boat, as John, Jr., in the stern swings his light toward shore, the eyes of the shrimp flash red with its reflection. His father in the bow casts the net again and again, every eight to ten seconds, bringing it in, emptying it, and casting it out once more. He wears khaki rubber overalls and black boots with a stripe of orange; on his head he wears a solar topee, incongruous beneath the moon. John, Jr., sits in the stern, lighting a Winston with one hand while with the other he maneuvers the rudder. He is dressed in sneakers and dark slacks, and a white-brimmed hat with a black band partially covers his dark features. Lean where his father is broad-shouldered and substantial, he plays basketball rather than football, Capricorn to his father's Cancer.

The water brought in with the shrimp washes backward through the boat with the same splash and wave as the water on either side—brown water with glints of scarlet and neon-white reflecting upward.

In the wood thicket not far from the landing, a female opossum makes her way through the brush and tangle of vines along the dark pathways. She moves from side to side, poking her nose and forepaws into the tangled roots that crisscross the damp earth. Her path each night is different from that of the night before as she digs for insects among the leaves. A night prowler, she spends her days in the hollow trunk of a lightning-struck oak. After sundown she emerges from the tree hollow, carrying with her in her pouch her dozen young that have lain next to her all day, suckling on her teats as she has slept.

At the water's edge she pauses, lifts her long nose up out of the marsh grass tangle, and makes a low hissing sound. There has been some movement in the marsh behind her, a toad moving in measured hops across dry leaves, but the sound is faint enough so that it arouses in her no more than a token registering of defense. She moves down into the water, as she does contracting the pouch-opening around her young—at sixty days still attached inside—keeping them completely dry. She glides quietly through the calm water, snatching every few feet at a water spider, a floating dragonfly.

From far behind her, in the deeper thicket of the pine forest, there comes the baying of a pack of wild dogs. She ceases her movement through the water at the sound, and rests with only her nose showing above the waterline. After the sound abates, she remains for a period of minutes motionless and alert.

In the boat John, too, listens to the sound of the distant baying. He frowns and he and his son exchange a glance in the darkness. Earlier in the month a pack of wild dogs had got into the pigs' enclosure at New Cut, killing three of the smaller animals and mauling two more. Most of the plantation's land is fenced off from the road, but the dogs manage more and more to break through the protection and worry the livestock. At present there are three sows and a single boar, plus a dozen or so piglets in the wooded yard. The two who have been mauled by the dogs are slowly recovering; John at midday throws them extra corn at feeding time. The white piglet's jaw has healed so that he is able to chew normally, while the injured grey piglet still totters on a ripped left hind leg and flank. Now they

sleep close to the sows in the cool muddy grass, one
or another of the group occasionally squealing drily,
thrusting out a hoofed leg in its sleep.

The boat drifts. John continues to throw out the
net, motioning slightly with his free hand when he
wants his son to change the boat's course. What talk
there is on the water is low and hushed. Voices carry
in the blackness; a whisper on the water may carry
for half a mile. There are no other boats out on the
Sound in the near distance; when other shrimping
boats do draw near and pass by, there is a soft greeting from each, familiar, relaxed. People who meet at
night know each other as much by their voices as by
their faces. Pale skin shines like neon in the southern
night; black men smile at one another in the dark.

The sky and the water and the mud flats between
are all part of the same cool black wetness. The
jumping of the shrimp creates a splashing sound like
that of a bubbling fountain. The boat moves along
the shoreline. A larger fish, a gar, is hauled in with
the shrimp and thuds into the hold, its tail slapping
the screen. John recasts the net, and the boat slowly
passes the mouth of Church Creek, then drifts out
again, angling northward. In three or four feet of
water, the disturbed shrimp light up and propel
themselves upward into the air; greyer in color than
the brown shrimp that have come through the
Sound in late April and May, they are the spawn of
those earlier shrimp. The summer's second generation is smaller, less robust—just as the corn fed to
the cattle and pigs is now the second crop, coarser
and less sweet than the earlier crop of the season.

The planting and flowering proceeds on Wadmalaw as the shrimp gestation proceeds in the water. In the fields soybeans follow wheat in the rich soil. Winter crops of cabbage and rutabaga follow spring and summer crops; there are three seasonal plantings in the island's gardens, as well. Okra grows to its fullest, then makes way for spinach and tomatoes. Beyond the big house, across from the grazing ponies, the tomatoes are soft and scarlet orange on the vine. Over the rows of curling plants and vines there are hung gourds which serve as nests for martins; at dusk the birds swerve and dive low over the garden, catching gnats and flies and midges.

The thud of the gar in the boat is echoed by the sound of a magnolia pod falling to earth near the water's edge. A pair of giant live oaks comes alive with every faint breeze that passes; every light stirring of the air moves the ropes of hanging Spanish moss. A rat snake slithers slowly along a bough, intent on a brown bat hanging head down among the ropes of blue-grey moss. The animal carefully, meticulously, licks its folded wings and legs. A moment before the reptile strikes, it flies off the branch and out across the water of the Sound.

The bat passes close down to the shoreline, within twenty feet of the moving boat, then cuts back across the wooded shore. John, Jr., watches its flight, turning slightly at the rudder. The path of the boat through the water now eases almost directly northward; John standing in the bow is lit by the faint light of Charleston at the muddy horizon. A small private plane on its way south to Savannah crosses through the arc of lighter grey, its two white lights and one red light blinking at intervals, its whirring engine too distant to be heard even in the echoing stillness of the marsh. At the shoreline a firefly lights up an inch or two of darkness, passing from the live oaks to a small cluster of pecan trees. There was a time when the property taxes of New Cut Plantation were paid by the nuts from these trees. That was back before the present owners, the Rutledges, came to live there—even before the earlier owner, Colonel Gambrill. John remembers when no automobiles traveled the dusty roads; a time of men and mules and boats. Against the blackness of the shoreline, the fireflies dot the air at intervals of two feet, each insect tracing an invisible line, a cool white dot, then another invisible line, along the shore.

John remembers the Depression, a time when all there was for a man to do was to shrimp at night, to try to keep body and mind together with what he could pull out of the water. That was the time of the old moss trucks traveling through the marshes and swamps, creaking along as men and women and children methodically stripped the Spanish moss from the limbs of oak and magnolia. Families lived by compressing the moss and piling it bale upon bale, and selling it for two cents a pound. After it was dried and twisted into cordage it was used for stuffing and horse collars, and in upholstery for furniture and carriages. The Depression lasted a long time in the islands and marshlands of the coastal South; the water and the shrimp are the same then as now, though the reliance on the livelihood they provide is less common. John's older daughters have recently bought him a new Ford XL 700, and he and his wife have moved off New Cut into their own home where they and their children and grandchildren live. John is an independent man, who has quietly worked all his life at maintaining his sense of freedom.

At fifty-seven, he moves and looks like a man in his mid-forties. He is reserved and powerful in the way that those who have worked all their lives, and were strong to begin with, are powerful. The power is quiet; the peace is earned. As he throws out the net, the sound in the air is only a slight tracing through the darkness. His shoulder stretches, pulls, and retracts; his strong arm moves, after the decades of night, with this same action, this same gentle casting, entirely on its own. During the day, his arm and shoulder have lately begun to give him some trouble, a stiffening and ache in the shoulder which he feels midday.

Between the ages of twenty-one and thirty-nine, John says he did everything and anything he wanted to do. There is nothing he feels he ought to have tried and didn't, nothing left unsampled that, given the opportunity, he'd like to try today. He thinks these are the years in which a man should do it all, so as not to set himself up in bitterness in his old age. What he wants to do now is simply keep on living, keep on providing in the way he has for those he loves. He has two twin grandchildren at home; they wait for him in the early evening so they can devil him once he walks through the door. His wife likes the company of their grandchildren, and she likes traveling up to New York to see the others. But traveling is not on John's mind much; there's too much work to do, too much on the land and water to keep him occupied. John, Jr., and Martha are both still in school, and there are expenses to be met to keep the son playing basketball at Orangeburg, to keep the daughter studying.

He remembers when the land sold for ten cents an acre to those who could buy; he remembers the war years and working at an aircraft factory. He wishes sometimes that he had had the opportunity to go to college, to take part in the life that his children have. Born on the island, he is tied to it as to family territory; his aunts and uncles have all come from the island, and he feels a pride in it, in its soil. He remembers his own grandmother, able without the benefit of eyeglasses to thread a needle at the age of 103.

The lantern is now lit in the bow, and the flame of burning gasoline underlights John's broad dark face. The smoke from John, Jr.'s, cigarette trails behind the stern; in the hold the shrimp pile up, their tail stingers and those at the maw slashing futilely in the wash of brown water.

The advice John most remembers his own father giving him was that he must never spend a night in jail. These years later, he maintains he doesn't even know where the local jail is, having abided by his father's advice all his life. Being locked up and confined is the worst situation he can imagine; he says those young men who snatch a bag or take some-

thing that doesn't belong to them, just so they can
get arrested and have a place to sleep and eat, are
beyond his understanding. The food is good
enough, but asking to be locked up is to him unnatu-
ral. He sees the young men on Market Street and
Broad Street, glassy-eyed and drifting; he thinks of
the time lost to them, their lives never really lived.
He feels both satisfied and fortunate in his own life,
no matter what the sadness has been, and wants his
children and grandchildren to live their lives as fully
as he has, in their own way, in their own time. He
sees differences in the generations, in the way they
respond to their own sense of self-preservation; the
younger children seem to him to be more resistant to
direction than their parents were, and won't out of a
sense of respect or duty alone obey their parents' orders. The children don't think so much of their own
physical survival, don't learn as quickly the defense
measures their parents have learned before them.
But it is, John says, a different world now, and he
supposes they'll get by all right. John, Jr., gently
guiding the tiller, watching the water, says nothing.
The night around them diffuses the immediacy of
them both, of their relationship and situation. The
water and the marshes are mute and the night air
falling on father and son falls on each differently.
For the one, the night is an arm of the future,
stretching, reaching out to undefined dreams; for
the other, it trails gently backward, touching the soft
body of the past.

Each night it is different, a slight veering in a
northeasterly direction, a circling in the Sound, but

each night it is the same: a path rebroken through the dark water. For three or four hours the boat moves on the current, gathering weight. Now it swings back across the deeper part of the channel, passing the blinking channel light. Above the men a star falls, disappearing just before reaching the water line. The men wonder about movement through space, about the feeling of traveling as an astronaut to the moon, or to the planets beyond. John laughs his low private laugh, and remarks that he hasn't nearly enough nerve to think of that kind of trip, that he wouldn't make it even halfway there.

John, Jr., turns off the motor, and the boat drifts in from the channel toward the shore.

On the muddy shore the female opossum is returning from the water, fatter by two mullets and a swarm of beetles. Tired from her exertion, and from carrying the weight of her litter, she proceeds with drooping tail and with paws that splay slightly outward in the sandy soil. She crosses the pine needle floor beyond the marsh thicket. Nearing the lightning-struck tree, she abruptly stops, just as the rasping sound of cicadas around her also stops. In front of her on the path a lone dog stands motionless, its jaws slightly opened, watching her approach. It is black against the blackness, a dark mongrel with a rust-colored muzzle, separated from the pack. As it moves toward her, beginning to bark as it lowers its head, she repeats the hissing sound she earlier used at the water's edge, but only for one exhalation of breath. Then she is on her side, fallen as if shot, her legs stiffened and splayed, her lips curled backward from her needle-sharp teeth. As the dog's wet muzzle closes on her, she lies motionless against the leaves. He picks her up and shakes her back and forth between his powerful jaws, then drops her to earth where she lies with tongue extended, eyes staring upward unblinking. Again he paws her, but steps back as urine and feces seep out of her body. She is without response, without feeling; in the few moments since sighting her attacker she has entered a state called apnea, an involuntary response that slows heartbeat and respiration, making both inaudible. She has the look and smell of a dead animal, and the dog, uninterested in a dead carcass, after a moment more of pawing turns and pads off past the oak tree, following a more interesting scent. The opossum remains motionless where she lies. Her body, rigid and foul in its comatose state, rests on its side as the animals within her pouch squirm at the teat. No movement from within shows through her furry flesh. After nearly a half-hour of this inactivity, she comes slowly back to life. She regains her feet and, before proceeding farther, licks her whiskers and her fur. At her normal rate of speed she then continues onward to her nest.

The boat returns to the dock. The circle around the Sound is completed, the shrimp in the hold are piled deep enough and thick enough for the men to bring them in.

Now the catch is weighed in the boat. There are, in addition to the shrimp, which measure about sixty pounds, two large horseshoe crabs, a few shad, and the slender gar in the hold. There are nights when John goes out fishing on consignment, filling up two thirty-pound buckets of shrimp for private parties. These are boiled or fried, or served in a variety of Carolina salads, slipped into sandwiches, or arranged artistically in crystal bowls and garnished with plumes of lettuce and lemon. Tonight is Friday night, though, and the catch is intended not for private buyers but for the public on Market Street on Saturday morning. The shrimp must be iced as soon as possible after coming out of the water, and there are tin tubs in the trunk of the Belvedere to carry them back to the house. There they will be packed in layers: three inches of shrimp covered by three inches of ice, with three layers of each per tub.

The boat washes against the dock at high tide; over the stretch of barnacles and mud over which John, Jr., poled hours before, there are now nine feet of water. Up and down the coast, larger boats and small boats are coming in. At this season, the shrimp are sold locally at $1.25 a pound; sea fishermen on party boats will be buying bait for the day's excursion, and there will be women who will buy only enough for the weekend, stuffing two or three pounds of the cool, crusty pink flesh into rope shopping bags, wedged in brown paper.

The men will be able to sleep for an hour or two before John makes the twenty-five-minute drive into Charleston, just before dawn. At five thirty, on Market Street, he will engage in good-natured and familiar competition with four or five other river fishermen set up in their cars. The fishermen make up a unit of cars, parked with trunks out facing the street, half a block from the stone church that marks the end of the fruit and vegetable stalls. It will be a warm dawn; the ice around the shrimp will melt quickly as the vendors and shoppers move slowly back and forth among the stalls. It will be a Saturday market day like many others before it; after it has passed, John will drive back to Wadmalaw, to take up the chores of the day.

John, Jr., steps out onto the wooden dock, secures the line, and steadies the tubs while his father separates the catch. Nearby, in the freshwater lily pond, the creatures beneath its surface bob upward, nudging the green pads apart, breaking the water line with wart-rimmed eyes.

Passing around the cattle barn on the far side of the pasture, the black dog pauses to investigate a movement next to the post fence. The movement is the easing awake of a mottled rattlesnake, moving slowly against the dry wood. It strikes as the dog snarls, before it can bark. When the barking comes, it comes in a howl of surprise and pain; the venom begins to circulate in the animal's system almost as soon as it breaks the skin. As the dog races across the dark pasture to escape the pain, to rejoin the other mongrels of the pack, its left leg falters. Not far from the main entrance gate, it pauses to lick the wound, to nip at the sting. It stops a few feet from the road, resting in the grass. John will discover it there, bloated and already some hours dead, when he drives the pickup truck through the pasture that afternoon.

The shrimp is piled in the tubs, and the tubs placed in the truck. The car is started, a gentle coughing in the darkness, and then the headlights

are turned on. Their two shafts of light pick up first
the lengths of hanging moss, the trees and the sloping barn, then as the car turns in its path, the wood
and shingle outbuildings adjacent to the big house.

From behind, looking in from the waters of the
Sound, the path of the car is a straight line moving
up along the dirt road, its lights receding, growing
smaller. They blink out at the first turning. On the
dock the sense of waiting softly reestablishes itself,
and the only points of light and movement are the
floating stars.

God and Man
in the Tenderloin

Every year at Christmas, Jonelle says, she lights a candle for Candy Darling. People in the district all have their patron saints.

The landscape of the Tenderloin is compressed, compacted and squeezed together like an aluminum bale in a scrap yard, with gaudy wires sticking out of the fissures. The Tenderloin exists to some degree in many towns; the one in San Francisco is the genre champion. Its boundaries are Market Street to the south and Geary Street to the north, with the cable cars of Powell to the east and an eight-block stretch of Hyde to the west. A cop is said to have remarked, when he found out he was moving to the downtown graft district, "Now I'll be eating tenderloin instead of hamburger." It is an old remark, and the current eateries feature a rather less ambitious menu. It's a tough life in the Tenderloin, and those who live and work there move about, in bars and cafés and on the street, in small squadrons of defiant sociability. The landscape is bleak, but at night the hard edges seem smoother.

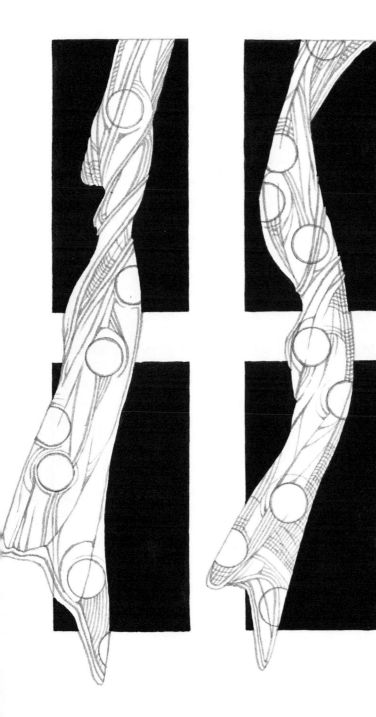

Don Stuart is an ordained minister and has been the night minister in the district for twelve years. He works four nights a week now, but when he started out he worked five and sometimes six; at that time the church program concentrated on putting teenage runaways back in touch with their parents. The ministry switchboard provided the only link between families, and Don says it was a means of bringing scores of people back together. The only other switchboard at the time was a suicide line; now various lines have proliferated and the network is relatively arcane.

Don goes to work at ten in the evening; the phone volunteers in his office on Mason Street arrive at nine thirty. In all, there are forty men and women who answer the phones over a period of a month. Don is out of the office more than he is in it, walking through the streets with his beeper, or driving. Most of the people who call in call because they have nowhere to sleep. Various churches contribute funds; Don says that ecumenical funding provides three thousand dollars a year for the ministry's use. The YMCA on Turk Street provides three free rooms a night, and the funding pays for additional rooms when necessary.

The week previous has brought seventeen calls on the Sunday, twelve on the Tuesday, nine on Wednesday. There is a downswing midweek; on the weekends the night is filled with people reaching out, asking for help, looking for one another. For the lonely and depressed, the weekends seem like

other people's holidays. In the bars lonely people
stuff telephone numbers into one another's boots. In
Chinatown they laugh in high hysterical voices,
writhing in front of plate glass mirrors. In North
Beach, they peer through the windows of the strip-
pers' dressing rooms.

Don says the pace of the ministry is sometimes tax-
ing, sometimes not. He finds that he relaxes best by
painting, and he looks forward to four hours every
Tuesday morning, when, after he has come home
and had a nap, and his wife has left for her German
class, he spends time at an easel, working in oils,
painting the sea. Don is fifty-four and looks ten years
younger; his is a beatific face in a beatific town. In
San Francisco social change and the moral sensibil-
ities of the times shift the focus of his activity; the
needs of youth are replaced by those of the aged.
Whiskey is replaced by heroin, and heroin by gin,
and then the pattern is changed yet again. Those
whose paths cross redemption are constant, however.

Paths intertwine like cat-gut threads, stitching
themselves across the concrete of the city streets.
Good intentions cast a diagonal across the path of
fantasy. Lust and death collide. A pause of a few
steps here and there alters the smaller rhythm, but
the larger rhythm remains the same; the pattern is
changed by the casting of random elements, like the
simple casting of the I Ching. Religions of body and
mind scrape against each other, reflecting more in-
tensely haphazard detail.

Don is a fixture in the night of the Tenderloin; his presence helps to hold up the weight of darkness. His job is to be there, and always to be there, when people call. His family has adjusted to his life; his son, Mark, works on the night desk at the Turk Street YMCA, part time, and is, like his father, at home in the night. The minister's wife is still a creature of the day; Eunice and Don have built their lives around the needs of the ministry, and the small compromises have only strengthened their own relationship. On their twenty-fifth wedding anniversary they took a long-postponed trip to Italy and stood together on Florence's Ponte Vecchio to exchange new rings to replace the thin bands each had worn since their wedding. A minister's wife is always at the mercy of circumstance; the list is long of parties unattended and concerts unheard because of a phone call in the evening, or the morning, or the afternoon. Now, with Don alternating nights with another minister, his family is able to make plans with slightly more security. Vacations are measured in hours and days, not weeks, never months. The family is divided by sex and biorhythm, with both Eunice and her daughter, Kathy, preferring the activity of the day and the two men, father and son, preferring the night.

A large red book rests on the desk of the ministry office. It is the Social Service Referral Directory, and it is used every night by the volunteers for non-emergency calls. There are charts on the wall of the rectangular mission room, and there are coffee cups stacked together near a hot plate. The mood is efficient and friendly. Don is sometimes called upon to show ministers from out of town his working situation, and a New Jersey minister now sits with him, sipping from a cup of coffee. A red-haired volunteer settles into the chair at the telephone desk; another younger man with him silently watches and listens as he takes a call from someone asking for the number of the diabetes hot-line. A call comes through from a regular, a woman who calls in at least twice a week, ostensibly to ask for advice about her son, who she says has a drinking problem. The red-haired man listens patiently, every so often agreeing with what she is saying. Another caller wants to know the number for Golden Gate Gay Liberation. The number is given, along with the admonition to call back if there is no response, or if there is anything further the caller needs.

A yellow sheet of paper is filled out each night, labeled NIGHT MINISTRY TALLY SHEET. After the space for the day and time, there is a grid of squares to fill in, depending on the type of call received. The priorities of the night are these:

Religious
Loneliness
Depression
Suicide
Psychological
Marital/Family
Drugs
Alcohol
Sex (as problem)
Medical
Criminal
Financial

Food
Servicemen
Police (from)
Housing
Legal

There is space to write down the sex of the caller,
the time of the call, and any other information, comments, or messages received. As often as not, more
than one box is checked for each call.

Don says that, naturally, some people try to take
advantage of the housing setup. He cites two college
girls who recently called the ministry, passing
through San Francisco on a hitchhiking spree. When
Don told them that other emergency cases needed
the rooms, the girls accused him of being un-Chris-
tian, and hung up.

There are repeaters who call in again and again.
They talk to different volunteers, depending on the
night they call, and their histories make up substantial files. One such repeater has called seventeen
times in one night. This is part of the ministry program, responding to calls that initially may seem triv-
ial but that are almost always symptomatic of something deeper. The night ministry number is
essentially a crisis number; many callers say they
have been referred to the ministry by their psychia-
trists, and anyone dialing the operator or information after ten with an emergency is given the number.

Canned food is dispensed; there are tins of hash,
tuna fish, and ravioli, lining the shelves off the main
room of the ministry.

Don says that since he's been in the Tenderloin, the area has been put through some extreme changes. The Yerba Buena urban renewal project has involved the relocation of much of the area's population of older pensioners and workers. These older residents have been moved out of the apartments in which they've spent the better part of their lives and been placed in hotels which were once for transients but which now cater exclusively to the aged and infirm. Most of these hotels are north of Market Street, and whereas the rent for a week south of Market was twenty-five dollars, now the rent is double that a few blocks north on Turk Street. The older residents, whether dispossessed or not, are still careful about their budgets, and food is their first priority, always. Although they are poor people in a poor district, Don says the old are still conscious of their pride, and the food from the night ministry goes to the young and dispossessed much more frequently than it goes to the elderly.

There are also churches, such as St. Boniface and St. Anthony's, where whoever comes in is fed. St. Anthony's dining room on Turk Street serves over a million free meals a year.

Don will see anyone who calls in and wants to see him, no matter what the circumstances, the first time. The phone is reassuring, but flesh and blood reassurance is sometimes what's needed most.

A call comes through from the auxiliary ministry office at the YMCA; a young man has just had his knapsack and sleeping bag stolen and has nowhere to go. He had been hitchhiking north; and the car that brought him into town sped off with all his worldly goods in the back seat as he stood groggy on the sidewalk. He is still incredulous; the man who drove off had talked to him good-naturedly for an hour and a half on the road.

Don says he will come over and talk to him, and maybe they can do something about his getting a room.

Jonelle wends her way through the night. Her face is drawn together by the intention of beauty. She has been in San Francisco forever, she says.

She says she has no schedule, that she gets up when she feels like it. She rents a room on Turk Street by the week, and lives alone most of the time. She clops along on her platform soles, looking in on the bar life, flipping through the magazines in the body book stores, sipping a root beer slowly through a straw at the counter of the Pam Pam restaurant.

Don leaves the ministry offices on Mason, accompanied by the Atlantic City minister, also named Don, and the two of them head south toward the YMCA. On the corner of Geary and Taylor, two Scientologists are handing out leaflets silently, in the manner of a middle-aged man a block away handing out his leaflets for Girls, Girls, Girls. The two ministers pass the young Scientologists as if they were invisible; the teen-agers for their part ignore the men in their collars, as they do the winos who hector them from bottle-littered doorways farther south.

DARE TO BECOME MORE YOURSELF

is the message of the blue leaflet.

The ministers pass a restaurant on O'Farrell Street

where a waitress is leaning over the counter, examining a chain which one of the men sitting there, a jeweler, has mended for her. The chain is a keepsake from her son, and she is happy to be able to clasp it around her neck. There are four men sitting together at the counter, each of them slowly eating a piece of banana cream pie. They are Italian and speak every so often to one another in a dialect shorthand. Three of them wear hats; one is bareheaded. They are all in their fifties, or sixties. A dancer from the Girls, Girls, Girls establishment next door comes in to order sandwiches and coffee to go; she is tall and red-haired, and looks around the restaurant as soon as she enters to see if there's anyone more interesting than the four men. Someone young. Someone snappy. There isn't; she remarks to the men that they'll all get fat eating pie. *I* never eat a bit of pastry, she says, patting her flat stomach. She is wearing a maroon sweater and slacks.

After the waitress hands over the bag of sandwiches and coffee, and the dancer leaves, she continues her conversation with the men.

One of the hatted men wants to know if she knows how long a generation is. "How many years is a generation?" he asks, in the way that older men do—straight-faced and smiling at the same time. The waitress thinks about it, then says ten years. She reconsiders and says no, fifty years. The hatted man is pleased to be able to set her straight.

"Thirty years is a generation. I used to think it was a hundred, but it's only thirty. Only thirty years for a generation. Ain't that something?"

The waitress nods her head that it is, then moves off to fill the sugar bowls and creamers on the vacant table. It is nearly closing time. The men eat slowly, as if in a race to see who will finish last. The jeweler from time to time tries to engage the other men in a conversation about clasps, but none of them has interest enough to reply. Finally, they finish their pie, and after saying good night one by one to the waitress, they file out the door. The waitress, alone now except for the cook in the kitchen behind, begins to lean the chairs against the tables in the back half of the room. Then she returns to her spot behind the counter, watching the night through the plate glass window, now and again touching the chain, humming to herself.

Don says raising children in the night is no less rewarding than raising them by day. His own two children grew up seeing him at odd hours, in the morning and the evening; other night workers arrange their leisure time to accommodate their young. A father drives his young daughter to kindergarten each day even though it's close enough to walk, just so he gets the fifteen minutes alone with her each morning. Another father wakes up at three in the afternoon to play basketball with his son for an hour before he goes off to work. Mothers who work at night don't get to attend many PTA meetings, but they are able to serve their children a leisurely breakfast before they go to sleep. Don says his wife, Eunice, and he are happy with his hours, that working nights is like gaining time in a way. He likens it to their stealing a few seconds each night from time, pushing back against its revolving band of movement of day to night to day.

The first light of the Bible was called Day; all

darkness was called Night. Biblical light extends past
solar light: in Genesis it says that the evening and the
morning were the first day. A day can be assembled
from either end.

The activity of Don's night is the activity of quiet
support. Around him flesh is peddled and eyes are
blackened and the denizens of the district slice small
bits from each other's wizened souls.

On the corner of Market and Turk, Don sees a
friend of his, a young hustler named Bobby. Bobby
is sandy-haired and his eyes are light blue. As he
talks to Don, his gaze is on the street. He shifts from
one foot to the other, smiling, laughing at something
Don says. Don talks with him alone; he says that
most of the street people he is in contact with are
wary of strangers, even collared strangers. Bobby is
married and has had a tough time with his wife in
the last few months. They both have a history of
heroin addiction, and although Bobby is now tech-
nically clean, he worries about his wife. She knows
he is turning tricks on the street, and sometimes it
gets her down. Bobby has served time in Illinois and
California and as an ex-con has difficulty finding
work. He turns up across from the big shoe store on
Market between eleven and two in the morning, and
he has some regular johns who pick him up. Like a
lot of hustlers, he says he is only in it for the money.
He prefers johns older than himself. Don talks with
him for ten minutes or so and then moves on.

There are people who are more open to sharing
than others, people who want to share their experi-

ence, their observations, talking to strangers, making new friends, engaging in small talk. And there are their opposites. The redemption of souls cut off from the common herd is not an easy business. Don's face has a certain detachment, for all its warmth, a certain objective glaze which has to do with the knowledge, after nearly fifty years, of the inevitability of statistics. There are statistics on venereal disease and on death, and there are probable and improbable suicides.

Don's wife has seen enough to know what to expect of her husband when he comes home from work. There are mornings when he is radiant and mornings when he is somber, but mostly he is matter-of-fact.

Don thinks that relating to people at night is different from relating to them by day. The Tenderloin at night is subtler; the people are not threatened by sunlight, by the long shadow of failed ambition more visible by day. Egos in the night are given more room to move around in. In barrooms they stand leaning on the only territory they know. Drinking is a release, an easing of the pressure of failure, an escape into an egoistic cocoon. In San Francisco deaths caused by cirrhosis of the liver are four times the national norm. Sloe gin spills on a wooden bar and drips like blood onto a sawdust floor. Men and women who live out of paper bags drink raw alcohol and witch hazel to sleep.

Other drugs in the city alternately numb and intensify. Alcohol addiction has increased in the last

five years, whereas hard drug addiction has de-
creased. There isn't a lot of cocaine in the Tenderloin; rich men's drugs are in short supply. There
is heroin, and there is methadone. Two weeks before, a welfare mother has mixed in methadone with
her baby's milk to put it to sleep, and the baby has
died while the mother slept on the couch a few feet
away.

In the bars on Folsom Street men trip and smoke
and drink beer. Pink passion and purple haze are
small pills that change hands frequently. There is
mescaline on Sutter Street and blotter on Castro.
Drugs come and go and some are more lethal than
others.

Jonelle says there is less sense of competition by
night. Men who have it drummed into them all day
long that they are failures can still pretend at night
that they are going to get on top of things, that
somehow soon they'll make a success.

Mack is a drinker of gin who coasts along through
the night, turning up in bar after bar, his brown
sweater mended at the collar, his tan poplin jacket
greasy at the elbow. As the evening passes, his features slide downward, collecting in a pile of wrinkles
and yellow flesh at the collar line. Mack is all right
with men, but as he drinks he tends to get ugly with
women. When it is a bad night, he maligns them
from across the room, loud and sarcastic, trying to
get them to respond. The women in the district generally know what they're doing and how to take care
of themselves. They ignore him, or they ask him
how he'd like his face pushed in.

Jonelle says guys like Mack are the ones who in the end just want you to hold them—tricks who, after they have taken you to their hotel rooms, or after you have taken them to yours, do not want to engage in any sexual activity whatever, but just want to be held in the dark. Jonelle says some of her customers cry after intercourse, especially the drinkers. It's always the drinkers, she says, who want to be held.

At a bar called the Old Crow on Market, the customers stand drinking screwdrivers and boilermakers and bottles of beer. Hustlers and their johns congregate at the bar, with much coming and going through the front entrance, out onto the sidewalk.

"That one's showing a lot of lunch."

Jonelle moves through the barroom, leaning over the tables, commenting on whoever crosses her path. Her voice is loud, but not harsh.

"Ummmm. Tasty." She laughs and moves on.

She thrusts her hip against a man in blue jeans and a leather jacket who stands at the bar and then, a second later, sees someone she knows outside on the street.

Jonelle has had her body embroidered in silicone; triangles and wedges of it have been meticulously stitched into her flesh. She says it's divine, that she loves being a concoction. She has had flesh added. She has had it removed. Her first operation, in Mexico, involved having a new chin installed when she was twenty-one. She says the doctor used the jawbone of a pig, or maybe it was some other bone, but it was definitely from a pig, she remembers. Later, there were some painful complications because of the tissue not meshing. Jonelle doesn't care. It's all been worth it.

She stands on the pavement, caressing the face of a young policeman who looks back into the bar from time to time, grinning as she speaks to him.

Jonelle is an independent who turns tricks when she likes, and only when she likes. She says she is twenty-nine, and no one disputes her. A half-hour after she has said she is twenty-nine, she takes a card case out of her bag and without a word points to the birth date, which shows her to be thirty-eight. The name on her birth certificate is Jonathan A. Vellassi.

The blond cop pulls himself away from Jonelle. He says he'll maybe see her later. He is still new to the beat; his partner catches up to him on the corner where Turk touches Market. They cross the street and proceed north, talking about the unresolved death of Sal Mineo and other homicides.

The two policemen pass the two clergymen and all nod a cursory greeting. The New Jersey minister is telling Don about the article he once read about him, in an old copy of *Presbyterian Life* magazine, and about how it got him started in his own night ministry. Each of the two ministers has constructed his life around the ministry; for the older man the details of the night are more a habit, a series of adjustments, while for the New Jersey man the contrast between night and day is still sharp. Don sleeps when he can. Four or five hours in the morning, a few in the afternoon; his wife and he get to close their eyes together on weekends, but not often during the week.

The glass door of the YMCA slides open and the men enter, stepping around a silent man holding a puppy in a cardboard box on the steps. The man has been selling dogs all night, some for five dollars, some for twenty. They are German shepherds, and their mother is whining through a bathroom door in a welfare hotel a few blocks away. The man, who calls himself Keno, sells the dogs before they are weaned, coming up to people on the street, mostly in the hours just before dusk, as they come home from work. He has his best luck with the elderly. He always says he is leaving town and has just been to the veterinarian to see about boarding the puppy, but that as it turns out he can't afford to pay the fee. He says that the dog needs a home, that it's purebred, and that he sure hates to sell him—or her—but that he must. At midnight all that is left is the runt of the litter, a whimpering female with tan spots.

Jimmie Johnson lies in his hotel room a block from Turk Street. His body has been collapsing from heroin for a period of years; the tie he has knotted around his arm, loosened now, is a tie he bought in Seattle when he was working there, loading and unloading crates of sardines, back during the fair. The tie is red with small white stars. Jimmie Johnson used to be a boxer, and his arms are still strong, with black flesh hanging loosely from the biceps. The veins are heavy and looped upon one another. The arms are rigid at the elbow, the fingers curled.

He dies at six minutes after midnight. His clock, grey and battered, which he has carried with him up and down the coast of California for thirty years, stops ticking eight hours later. He has wound it two mornings before, hungry and agitated, waiting for his pusher to come around with his medicine. The medicine, heroin, is badly sifted; the liquid he sticks into his arm moves through the network of his veins too far too fast. And he is dead. His pusher learns of his death a week later, and of the deaths of two other men. He flies to Chicago and starts calling himself by a different name.

It has all happened before.

Inside the YMCA a woman with the name Foxy on a platinum chain around her neck is standing by the main desk. Don watches her out of the corner of his eye while he talks to the boy who has had his knapsack and sleeping bag stolen. The boy is eighteen and has come all the way from Vermont; he says the pack was worth $150, and that the sleeping bag was stuffed with down. He has a red bandanna around his neck, which he keeps twisting as he talks to Don. He is near tears. Don sets him up at the desk with a free room for the night, and the boy, in a kind of daze, takes the key and walks toward the elevators in the back.

Foxy is trying to check into a room for the night, but every time the clerk asks her her name, she says it's none of his business. Her movements are slow and awkward, and at one point she drops her large red purse onto the floor, where it spills out a can of Arrid Extra Dry, a pay envelope, a fifty-dollar bill,

and half a dozen handkerchiefs. She asks the clerk
for a cigarette, then says she doesn't want one and
stoops to pick up the contents of her purse. She
laughs to herself as she replaces the handkerchiefs.

The clerk again asks her to give him her name so
that he can check her in, but she won't do it. After a
while, not saying anything more, she moves slowly
toward the door, and then back out onto the street.
The man with the dog has gone, and she stands
alone on the steps until she decides to walk east.

Coming from the Old Crow, Jonelle hurries along
toward a date she has made earlier in the night with
a man from Tucson who is planning to open up a
bathhouse to replace the downtown Barracks. He's
told her to meet him at the YMCA lounge. Jonelle
thinks of herself as an entertainer of sorts. She
thinks the new bathhouse should have entertain-
ment, and she thinks she should be it. She can mime
any number on the jukebox, she says, and she knows
how to show-dance.

She is wearing a silk Korean jacket over her
sweater and slacks, and she snaps and unsnaps the
buttons as she trots along. Ahead of her she sees
Foxy on the street.

She calls out to her from half a block away.

"Girl, where did you get that heaven coat?"

Foxy stands very still. She watches Jonelle approach, not replying until she is standing next to
her. She is not sure she knows her; she is not sure
she knows anyone, but the mention of her new coat
brings her back to a semblance of reality.

"My old man gives me a new coat every holiday.

He says I deserve a change of skin." She laughs at
herself and does a clumsy pirouette in front of Jonelle on the sidewalk, spreading the lapels of the short
rabbit coat as she moves in a slow circle. Underneath, she is wearing gold hot-pants, with a pair of
red and black felt hearts embroidered on the side.
"You looking real good, honey," says Jonelle. "You
looking like a million bucks. Your old man sure must
be sweet to you." Jonelle doesn't use junk, and she
knows it never does any good to talk to the girls like
Foxy who do. She also knows Foxy's old man has put
her in the hospital two months before with a broken
hip.

She leaves Foxy and continues on her way to the
Y. A car slows down on the dark street and then
speeds up again. It circles the block and, when it
again reaches the spot where Foxy is standing, stops
across the street from her, idling its engine, dimming its lights. Jonelle turns and sees that the car has
out-of-state license plates, and that Foxy can barely
make it across the street. She crosses over and comes
up to the driver's window on the street side. She sees
that there are two men in the back as well as the
driver in the car. As Foxy leans against her shoulder,
she takes her arm and pulls her away, up onto the
sidewalk.

"Listen, baby. You want to lie down for a while up-
stairs. Come on. I'll take you up; you close your eyes
for a while." She pulls her along and turns the corner; the car accelerates with a screech on the damp
pavement. The men in back sit up as it turns the
corner onto Market.

Jonelle's apartment is small and cluttered. There

are dishes in the sink, and sheets of tissue paper pinned together in piles on a formica coffee table. There is a cat, somewhere. Foxy is barely awake as Jonelle pulls her legs up on the couch and stuffs a pillow behind her head.

"Make sure you lock the door if you go out, now. Okay?"

Foxy sleeps, and Jonelle sits in an overstuffed chair by the window, looking out and down at the street. She lights a Kool, inhales deeply, and opens the window an inch or so to let in a little air.

Jonelle feels as if somehow she's off her stride tonight. The night can pass in a flash of humor and passion, or it can lie before her, dumb and resistant. She finishes her cigarette and quietly puts on another sweater under her jacket. Then she stuffs another half-dozen calling cards into her purse. She changes her embossed profession from time to time, largely on the basis of whim. The card now reads:

MISS JONELLE
Custom-Made Men's Ties

The two ministers pass out of the YMCA lounge as Jonelle passes in. The men who come in for rooms now come in pairs. An old white-haired man with a cane sits in a torn vinyl chair watching the desk, every twenty minutes hobbling to the front door to look into the street.

Jonelle sits down in the lobby without a word. She waits for her entrepreneur-date for a half-hour, then gives up. Pulling her silk jacket around her, she walks back out onto the street. Damned if she's not going to redeem the night somehow.

Don says he always tries to listen to some music in the night. The two ministers drive in his Pinto to a club called the QT, where a friend of his named Ann Farrell sings the blues. They stop in for only two numbers and then are called by Don's beeper back to the Y, where a couple from New Mexico has appeared with their infant son, looking for lodging, unable to pay. The men leave the club as Ann is midway through her second set of the evening.

"You went away and my heart went with you,
I speak your name in my every prayer. . . ."

Ann is a secretary by day; at night she sings in the club—two sets, drinks in between. She has a melancholy manner; she and Don have been friends for a long time. Her voice is strong and sweet. In the blue spotlight her face is like a floating valentine. Men and women pick each other up at the bar; the majority of the patrons are male. There are streamers and balloons hung about, suggesting Mardi Gras, New Year's Eve, Hallowe'en. The bartender reaches beneath the counter and places a black rubber bat in the palm of a regular customer, along with his change. The customer shrieks with horror and delight, and then the two look sheepishly at Ann, who continues to sing, never interrupting her mood or her metre.

White hookers congregate on Taylor and Turk; black hookers stand together on the corner of Turk and Jones. Turk Street smells of onions at 1:00 A.M. The street is grey. Looking down from the window of the YMCA a boy from Provo, Utah, who has been staying there a week, feels, suddenly, that it is all too grey, too dark. He takes his cigarette lighter and lights the bottoms of the flimsy cotton curtains that hang in his window. The material is cheap, and old; the window is instantly framed by two columns of fire. He laughs happily at the sight.

On the seventh floor a visiting bartender from Chicago, pulling on his boots for a walk down to Howard Street, sees a thin trickle of blue smoke coming through the boards of the floor next to his bed. He picks up the phone and tells the desk clerk on the ground floor what he sees.

The fire is extinguished by the night security man; the boy from Utah is taken to St. Joseph's Hospital, where he is placed under observation in a long room painted pale green.

Seagulls gather on the roofs of Tenderloin buildings at three thirty. On Market Street the signs in all-night neon are predominantly orange and pink and white. Men sleep in the doorways of the Civic Center, muttering and cursing at the pavement, at the world, from their sleep. Cochran's Pool Hall has not yet locked its doors; a game of snooker ends, and then another is begun. Blue chalk is rubbed slowly on the blunt ends of cues; the balls are racked and racked again.

In the window of Wig World, a blonde head revolves through the night, slowly turning in the midst of stationary brunettes and redheads.

Warren from Chicago returns to his room alone; the bars have not been crowded this week-night, and the excitement of finding the fire in the room below him has been the main event of his evening. In the lobby below, the young parents huddle together with their baby on the vinyl couch as Don talks to them. He says there is no problem. It used to be that only couples who were married could check into the Y, but now marriage is no longer a prerequisite.

Men rent hotel rooms for ten dollars a night in the Tenderloin; they sit on the side of the bed with their clothes on, staring at the grey walls.

The old white-haired man with the ebony cane wants to talk to Don about sports, about a long skinny black runner from Ethiopia he once saw compete. Don slowly disengages himself and moves into the YMCA's auxiliary ministry office to the left of the main desk. Don Bitzer is yawning now; with the couple and their baby put to bed, Don urges him to go to sleep as well, saying that he has probably seen as much of the night as he needs to. The younger minister acquiesces. Each has gotten used to closing his eyes in solitude.

Alone in his office at 4:00 A.M., Don realizes that he has not yet eaten and leaves the building once again to walk across to the Pam Pam restaurant on Geary and Mason.

Jonelle sits two booths away, dipping french fries into a pool of catsup. She sits with the blond policeman she has met earlier; between bites she tells him that she wouldn't dream of him paying for the meal, or for anything. She says she feels positively incandescent.

Bobby watches the dawn come up from his spot underneath the marquee of the vacant Golden Gate Theatre. The windows of the Hav-A-Java coffee shop reflect the sky as it slowly lightens. He is alone and it is cold. The cruising police cars that appear periodically don't give him or the other hustlers any trouble at this hour. He walks to the corner of Geary, then back again, and when he regains his station, a car stops beside him. The driver leans across the seat and rolls down the window to ask where Castro Street is. Bobby puts his hands against the car door and lowers his head to face the driver. He says he'll show him the way if he likes. The man, without saying anything further, pushes open the door and Bobby slides in, across the seat.

Don sips his last cup of coffee of the night, his watchful gaze following the animated woman and her companion as they walk past him to the cashier's desk. The morning waitresses are coming on for their shift, bright-eyed women in gingham uniforms with starched napkins above their left breasts.

He pays the cashier, then steps back out onto the sidewalk. He imagines for a moment that he smells the salt air of the sea, but then the next moment the rough wet smell is gone, absorbed by the city and the streets.

In a house on Geary Street, a grandmother from Canton pushes back the draperies of her small cubicle of a room and, with the first light of day, begins her chanting.

Chicago Ed

The voice is warm, young, male; the tone is substantial yet light. It is midnight in Chicago, a cold hour in a cold town, and the voice spreads out over the city and its suburbs, balancing the icy force of Lake Michigan, easing the sting of the driving wind and snow.

In the cold Chicago night the wind whistling in off the Lake worries the downtown buildings and suburban houses, whirling around the concrete and glass spires of Michigan Avenue, battling cars and pedestrians, filling every pocket of air with numbing cold. The wind whips the snow about, everything is peppered white. Concrete earth blends into pale sky with no discernible horizon. Buildings seem to float in the midst of the torrent, just so many straws in the wind. Downtown, the pride of Louis Sullivan, Clinton Warren, and John Wellborn Root, stand buffetted alongside newer, less substantial structures; the earth floats, the city floats, and the elements rule.

This is Ed Schwartz, the voice announces. *Tonight we're all going to have a good time . . . tonight's the night for my totally unscientific, noncomputerized date-matching service. Women only this morning; you gals out there who need a man in your life, you call in, let me know what you're looking for, and we'll see what we can do. On the level. The man of your dreams is out there somewhere, let's put you and him together . . . we're going to start taking calls in a little while, we're going to find you beauties some company. . . .*

The man behind the voice thrusts his hand up as he talks, cuing a commercial spot for the Chicago Bulls, an ad for a seafood restaurant in Evanston. Outside on Michigan Avenue the traffic thins and few pedestrians battle the cold. Michigan Avenue is too long, too wide, for purely human commerce. In the snowy night it seems, more than ever by day-light, a stage set for the elements. To stand on the corner of Michigan and Ohio at midnight or 3:00 A.M. is to endure a lesson in human frailty—the same may be said for Ashland and Cossitt in LaGrange, Lincoln and Howard in Skokie, or a thousand other Chicago crossroads. It is all the same wind, all the same icy air. A few blocks west, patrol cars cruise through the snow and slush down North Clark Street; a lone bus crawls the same route, slowly, in fits and starts like an ice-encrusted tortoise. The street is lined with gin mills and used car lots and showrooms. In one Buick salesroom a shiny four-door model is advertised as The Messiah and has a bumper labeled He Who Loves Me, Follows Me. The showroom is neon-lit till dawn.

Clark Street drunks fall out into the unloving

night; old men and young men hold each other up,
finding shelter in phone booths with no phones, in
doorways with no handles.

A voice, the voice, is what's important. The voice,
more than body, face, hands, or mind, is the presence, is who Ed is. In the studio, watching the face as
it frowns or laughs and the hands as they illustrate a
point (hovering in the air, pushing a pencil back and
forth, waving a signal at the program's producer in
the next room), seeing the full chest, the full body
twisting as it swivels in its chair, one sees features
and gestures that are merely background; one realizes how little they signify. It is really only the voice
that matters. Warm—if it were a color, it would be
something like honey brown—and with a contained
mirth, it can still be serious without sounding somber. It confides. It is a snug voice, a voice that fits
perfectly in one's ear.

It reaches out across the night. Three sisters listen
in Downers Grove, in front of a stucco fireplace, with
a metallic log on the fire. White bakelite radios on
checked tablecloths in Berwyn kitchens; a walnut living room console in Zion; car radios ranging from
Kenosha to Terre Haute; AM-FM portables in dark
warehouses, police stations, all-night supermarkets,
gas stations, Pizza Huts. The voice lives less in the
throat of its owner than in the space between the
glowing orange tubes of each wood and metal
speaker through which it flows. It belongs wherever
it exists, at the end and not the beginning of its elec-
tronic journey. It is alive in a way that a photograph
of a native in the Philippine bush is alive. Marjorie

Fagan, intent on her piecework in Western Springs, does not actually believe there is a little man in her Sony box, does not credit the radio beside her press with a living, breathing presence. Yet she smiles at its jokes and nods toward it in agreement with its opinions.

The voice, it must be said, has a life of its own.

It's twenty-two degrees at Midway, twenty-four at O'Hare, and there's eight inches of snow on the ground at Midway. . . . The snow ordinance is in effect . . . the city can put a hook on your Edsel and tow it away, be careful now. And be kind to each other out there.

A song by the Carpenters, then another spot for a Bloomfield charity auction. The phone begins to light up; women are beginning to call in. While the record plays Ed answers the calls, tells them to hang on. (On the night of the date-matching service women call in and tell Ed briefly on the air what they want in a man. They leave their phone numbers with him, off the air, and on the air are given a code number by which they can be identified by subsequent gentlemen callers.)

The first call comes on the air at 12:33 A.M.

The woman calling in is nervous, has never used the service before, and seems self-conscious about doing so now. She tells Ed she is a nurse, working at night at Kenosha Memorial Hospital, across the Wisconsin border on the north shore.

A nurse, says Ed, and puts her at her ease by asking his standard nurse question: *What is the smallest bone in the human body? That's right, the stapes bone in the ear, you're a nurse all right, Sharon . . . now, how old are you, and what are your interests—besides toting bedpans—and how old a man are you looking for?*

Sharon's voice relaxes as she answers. She is twenty-one and loves to cook, especially Italian food, most especially lasagna. She loves horseback riding, and the outdoor life in general, likes going on picnics. She wants someone from twenty-one to twenty-seven. Doesn't care if he's blond or dark-haired, needs to be fun-loving but mature. An outdoorsman, a sport.

You'll find him, says Ed. *He's out there tonight, listening to your voice . . . he'll be calling in, don't you worry. That's our number one caller this morning, lovely Sharon, nurse and lasagna maker. . . .*

The next caller is eighteen years old and works as a radiology technician in North Chicago. Blonde and blue-eyed, she tells Ed she likes sports, especially volleyball, and identifies herself as Lee Ann. Her voice is high and rather thin; she seems to choose her words more carefully than the first caller, almost as if she's rehearsed them. She is not, she says, looking for a husband yet; she wants to wait until she's fully mature, until she's been around some more, before she marries. It's wrong to marry young, she thinks. She wants to wait, not rush into anything, not make a mistake. . . .

Ed listens, coaxing out her remarks on maturity, agreeing with her, getting her to say what she wants in a man. Not too old, not yet; she'd like to meet men between eighteen and twenty, who are tall and dark. Just for now. Ed smiles, the voice smiles. *Sure, okay, Lee Ann, just for now, not too serious just yet . . .*

*all you tall, dark, and handsome gents who like volleyball
. . . Lee Ann is number two, waiting for your call. The
rules are, you men wait until the women have all called in,
then call me here and I'll check you out. Remember the
number of the girl who turns you on, and we'll see what
magic we can do. . . .*

The next call is someone who's called in on a previous date night. The voice is husky, somewhat
breathless. Ed recognizes her: *Pearl from Westmont,
right? How you doing, Pearl? . . . What's shaking out
there in Westmont?*

Pearl replies that not much at all is happening in
Westmont. She explains that she is a Star Trek nut,
that she'd like to meet someone who looks like Wil-
liam Shatner but would in a pinch settle for Leonard
Nimoy. She's nineteen years old, five foot eight
inches tall, and a blonde.

Is that natural blonde or bottle blonde? Ed wants to
know. Natural, all natural, she answers. . . . I'm a
natural woman, Ed. *Of course you are, Pearl; now,
seriously, what qualities would you like in a man? . . .*

Someone who understands women, Eddie, that's
all I want. It is almost as if another woman is now
talking, so changed is Pearl's tone of voice; from soft
and bubbly to no-nonsense, a good ten years older
than the Star Trek nut. I had kind of a rotten child-
hood, Eddie, my family used to put me down a lot. I
wasn't very happy at home. I just want someone I
can trust, someone who'll understand me, that's all. I
don't care so much about age—say twenty to twenty-
four years old. Someone nice, someone who'll treat
me right, I guess.

Fine, Pearl, fine . . . we'll see what we can do. . . . No swine need apply, right Pearl? . . . Right . . . thanks for calling in, dear, bye now. . . . It's one ten in Chicagoland . . . cold and windy out there. . . . Let's hear something warm from the Beatles: "Michelle." . . .

While the record plays, Ed dials the fire department. He also has a direct line to the police department and the highway department. *What's burning?* he asks the fire department, and then smiles as he hears there are no fires reported, a very rare situation in Chicago on a winter night.

Back on the air: *This is WIND. Everything's calm and cool out there in Chicagoland . . . all you citizens are behaving yourselves . . . keep it up, keep it up. . . . Now let's take another phone call from another lovely lady . . . number four is coming up.*

Number four is Henrietta from Westchester, calling in for the first time. Her voice seems young, light, a singer's voice. She announces immediately that she is fifty years old and tired of sitting at home. I'm five foot five, a real blonde, and I've got hazel-blue eyes; I was married a long, long time ago— don't ask how long—and I've just started going out again. I'm full of life, Ed—life begins at fifty, you know, it really does. I love life and good fun. I like to go bowling, and I sing with a barbershop group. I love to eat—anything as long as it's food—and I'd like to meet a man between forty and sixty—how's that, Ed?

That's terrific, Henrietta, terrific . . . you sound like a happy lady. Thanks for calling in, dear.

All the phones are lit up; Ed adjusts the microphone and the telephones on the console before him. The table is covered with shiny black microphone cords coiled around each other, the silver mesh heads erect and facing outward, identical snakes, identical mouths. When Ed speaks into the wire head, his lips graze it, barely touching it. *That's number four, Henrietta in Westchester . . . number five coming up. . . . Speak up, my love, tell us who you are. . . .*

Ann of LaGrange Park is bashful; her voice threatens to break as she gives her name, explaining that she has never, never done anything like this before. She works as a secretary, downtown, riding the train in every day. She loves the train ride, she says, and pauses, not knowing what else to say.

How old are you Ann? . . . come on, now, don't be bashful . . . tell us what you look like, let the men out there know who you are. . . .

I'm an active girl. I've got dark brown hair and eyes, and I'm five foot one—I always say five foot one and one-half 'cause it makes me feel taller. I'm not just a secretary, I work as a dance instructor, too. And I like the good old hold-me-tight dances. I like to dance gently. Sometimes I like to play dealer's choice. I take an occasional drink; not too much, though, just when I'm out.

How old are you, Ann?

Since I feel young, I'd like someone younger—I don't want to watch TV all night. It seems like the men my age have all slowed down. You know, once you slow down you can't get back up again. . . . I'm fifty-seven, Ed.

*Fifty-seven years young, that's what you are, Ann . . .
do you cook, Ann? . . . I asked a lady last week what her
best dish was, and she said Corning Ware . . . what's your
best dish, Ann?*
Oh, there's so many; I do love to cook. Let's see—
maybe stuffed squash. I'm Lebanese, and I do a lot
of Lebanese cooking. What else—I almost forgot, the
man I'm looking for—it would be nice if he was an
Arthur Murray dancer. They're the smoothest, you
know.
*They'll be calling, Ann. Don't you worry. Keep on listen-
ing. Good night, Ann.*

Cindy, a press-punch operator from Carpen-
tersville, is nineteen, a bowler, a horseback rider,
brown-eyed and brown-haired, who didn't care
much for high school, and who likes going out to
rock concerts. The last one she went to starred
Wayne Cochran. Her last date was over two weeks
ago. Ed wants to know why she hasn't been out with
her last date since; *what was the matter with him,
Cindy? Was he one of those international types . . . was he
one of those guys with Russian arms and Roman fingers?*
Cindy's response is delighted giggles, light as snow-
flakes, light as youth; Ed's voice acts as a feather,
teasing, tickling. *Is that right, is that what the problem
was, Cindy? Don't you worry, we'll get you an honorable
gentleman this time . . . on this show we stress class, not
crass. . . .*
There is another spot for a used car agency, a
public health message on VD control, and then Ed
holds the calls while he plays an Elvis Presley single
from 1970, "Kentucky Rain." The singer's voice

takes over from Ed's, acting as a soft aphrodisiac, alternating syrup with staccato, the little boy in the
singer's voice loosening up emotions, easing them
out into the open. Ed lets it work, accepting a cup of
coffee from the show's young producer, checking
fire and accident statistics, looking up the day in history, punching hold buttons, humming along with
the music all the while so as not to break the vocal
thread entirely.

In the studio, machines hum and circuits light up.
In the tape room the large modern consoles face cas-
settes racked on columns that turn like paperback
book stands. Each column represents a year—from
the sixties, the seventies, even the late fifties—
stacked one on top the other: Dylan on the Penguins
on Patsy Cline on the Beatles. The console lights are
squares of red and blue and green; in the outer hallway there is a multicolored jukebox lit with flowing
primary colors day and night. Walking past it is like
passing the wizard's mouthpiece in Oz.

It's still snowing out there, I know, but don't abuse the
heating equipment in your house . . . turn it down when
you go to bed . . . keep each other warm. Caller number
seven coming up . . . hello, my lovely.
Nora from the South Side talks about how she
never communicated much at home, how she hopes
she's a better mother to her three and four-year-old
than her mother was to her. She is twenty-nine, five
foot five, with dark hair in back that's blondish in
front, bottled, of course. Ed cues in applause imme-

diately after she mentions her hair; wild applause, cheering, a reward for telling the truth. . . . She goes a little deeper; I don't need a man who's handsome or rich now; I just want an ordinary average person. Just so he's not a bum. I was married three and a half years ago, and divorced a year and a half ago. So I made a mistake, and now I've got the kids, and it's not so hot running around. This time I know what I want and what I don't. I thought I'd call you up and give your system a try. What's to lose, right?

Nothing to lose, Nora, everything to gain . . . that's Nora on the South Side, number seven. . . . Hello, number eight.

Valerie is twenty-six, a pediatric nurse, a frosted blonde with blue eyes who loves the songs of Barry Manilow. Ed asks her the stapes question, which she answers correctly.

I work in North Chicago. I spend my days chasing kids around the office; there are eight thousand patients in and out of the clinic I work in, Ed. When I get home at night, I've had it. Still, I go out to the singles bars. I don't know why I keep going, honestly . . . a guy buys you a drink and he thinks he's in.

Ed asks her how old Mr. Right ought to be.

You know, this'll sound corny, but I really don't judge people by age anymore. . . . Let's just say, no babies need apply.

You see kids all day, Valerie . . . how do you feel about your own? Do you think you'd be a good mother?

Valerie laughs, easily, amused. Not tonight, Ed. Then she adds, However, I *am* willing to discuss the matter. More laughter.

At ten of two Ed does an announcement for upcoming bake sales in various suburban parishes and
then follows it with a Howard Cosell impersonation.
The news comes on at two; there are ads for
Chryslers and Ramblers interspersed with sports
news. At the end of the news Ed plays "The Whif-
fenpoof Song."

Caller number nine identifies herself as Bea from
Mundelein. She is older than Henrietta but younger
than Ann: fifty-four. Blonde, blue-eyed, five foot
seven. And she likes a good time. I'm an awfully
good cook, you name it, I'll cook it, she says proudly.
She's used to the telephone, she talks freely, good-
naturedly. But I'd rather go out for dinner the first
time, she says. Then, after I know what sort of man
I've got—I can judge his stomach better.

After Bea there is an Eisenhower quote stressing
brotherhood, freedom, and the right to knowledge,
and then Ed puts through a call to Snowflake, Ari-
zona, where earlier in the week there have been reports of a UFO upsetting the local citizenry. The
deputy sheriff is cordial and Ed manages to find out
that there are six men taking lie detector tests, and
that he, the deputy sheriff, believes they definitely
did see something peculiar. No firsthand accounts,
though; it seems the young man who claimed to
have been taken aboard the craft is no longer in
Snowflake.

Ed's attitude, on the phone and on the air, is a
perfect blend of interest and skepticism. *Maybe it's so,
maybe it's not . . . keep your eyes on the skies out there, if
you see anything more, let us know. . . .*

Back to dating: *Tonight is for women only, next week we'll interview you men on the air, and then let the women decide what you all sound like . . . but no men tonight, except of course when the women are through calling in, and you guys want to call me to get their phone numbers. Remember, class, not crass, and serious gentlemen only. No funny stuff.*

Donna from Darien calls in to say she's especially partial to firemen. She's thirty-three years old, five eleven, and is yet another blue-eyed blonde (Ed has stopped asking about the bottled or real variety). She works as a Trouble Clerk in retail clothing and likes art galleries and classical music concerts. Her voice is very much in control of itself, almost prim. She admits to not having been downtown in over two years. She doesn't seem to need a man whose cultural tastes match hers; in fact, she says she prefers the outdoor type, someone who plays hockey and football. She is divorced, with one son eight years old.

Now, you're a divorced woman, Donna. I wonder if you've got any advice for girls who are about to get married, or are thinking about it. . . . Any tips? . . . Any mistakes you made that they might profit by? . . .

I don't know, Ed . . . I think, in some ways . . . I think I should have been a little bit smarter about having a family. I love my son . . . but . . . he came a little earlier than we thought he would. My husband courted me for six months before we were married . . . I'm speaking frankly, now . . . and he said he was taking care of things and, well, he wasn't. I'm thirty-three, right? Well, sometimes I feel as if there's a big chunk out of the middle of my life, and

I've got to go back and fill it in. I want someone to help me fill it in.

What has seemed prim in Donna's voice is now heard as something else: as if discipline and melancholy had squeezed together on one emotional track. Ed's response is to the melancholy: *There are a lot of good times out there, Donna . . . and I appreciate you talking about yourself . . . the more you let people see, the more there is for them to love . . . right? Anyhow, all of you fire chiefs out there, sitting around with nothing to do tonight, remember, Donna's number eleven . . . and now, Donna, this is for you and all the other gals on the line . . . a beautiful song in any language, and by now it's been recorded in almost all of them . . . here it is in English, Morris Albert's "Feelings."*

The next caller is a charmer. Her name is Suki; she describes herself as an egg-roll junkie. She works in Service Administration, is five foot seven and one-half and a Pisces.

How do Pisces and Taurus get along, Suki . . . the bull and the fish; doesn't sound too terrific, does it . . . so you're fond of egg-rolls, too . . . what else do you like, and do you like to cook?

Suki replies, The only ethnic dish I can manage is sweet and sour pork, Ed; mostly I cook American. I love fish, being a Pisces of course, except for gefilte fish. . . .

Laughter from Ed; he pushes a button and cues in groaning sounds. Then the opening bars of the Batman theme. *So what are your interests, Suki? What kind of fella you looking for? And, before we forget, how old are you?*

Twenty-nine, and I'd like a mature man, between thirty-five and forty. Someone with a few ideas in his head; I'm interested in anthropology, I try to keep up with Margaret Mead, I think she's a fantastic person. I like sports, poker, pool, nothing too strenuous. I'm divorced; I left my husband because there was no real communication there. I guess I'm sort of independent. And I love your show, Ed, and the music you play, especially Johnny Mathis. . . .

Ed's hands are immediately moving in the air, signaling through the glass to the control room. His message taken, his instructions heeded, he says, *Then this is for you, Suki, just because you're an egg-roll junkie like me.* . . .

Strings and French horns and a voice like deep pile carpet: Johnny Mathis plucked from the cassette rack, singing "Gina." As the song plays, Ed smiles to himself, pleased with the segue, pleased that the transition has been made from Donna to Suki, and that the show has lightened again.

Ed moves on to caller number fourteen, Kathy from the West Side who has a slight drawl. I'm twenty-three and five eleven and a half . . . and what I want is somebody good-looking . . . maybe not movie star handsome . . . but I would definitely like to spend time with somebody good-looking. . . . I've just gotten a divorce after three years, and it was a real mess. The one thing I can't handle is another drinker, Ed . . . my husband was an alcoholic and there just wasn't anything to do for him. I have a little boy three years old, and a daughter who's two, and I'd prefer a man between twenty-five and thirty. And I guess he doesn't have to be all *that* good-looking. . . . And, Ed, I wanted to tell you how nice it is listening to your program at night. . . . I just love the sound of your voice. . . . Bye now. . . .

Thank you, Kathy, thank you very much. . . . Nice to know we're appreciated out there, dear. . . . That's Kathy on the West Side of town, looking for a good-looking guy who doesn't live in a bottle. . . . Plenty of them out there, Kathy. . . . In an hour or so we're going to start taking calls from the men, so all you women, hurry up and tell us what you want. . . .

After the three o'clock news, there is a short station editorial on abortion, then another call to the firehouse at three ten. Still no fires.

Mike, the sound engineer, is moving back and forth in the control room, shaking off the middle-of-the-night inertia. The producer is elsewhere, lost somewhere in the labyrinth of rooms and small studios that make up the station complex. Outside the air is calm, the snow silent. The tone of night has altered, subtly, quietly. It is now deep night and the mood is reflective, the darkness turning upon itself and taking stock. At three o'clock souls slip away, into darkness and sleep, and sometimes death and insanity, but more often than not, merely into boredom.

It's the middle of the night in Chicagoland. . . . I hope you're all still with me out there . . . we've still got a lot of sociable females on the line . . . how about let's talk to some more.

The next call is from Michelle in Cicero, a part-time insurance worker with two children. Five foot four. Blonde. I'm stuck here in Cicero, Ed. Me and the kids. I was married for three and a half years . . . it didn't work out, but I'd definitely get married again if it was the right guy. . . . I like outdoor stuff, and he should like that too, I guess. . . . No married men, please.

There won't be many calling in, don't you worry, Michelle . . . did you hear your song I played earlier . . . Michelle, ma belle? . . . Give us a little kiss on the air, dear, nobody's given old Eddie a kiss all night. . . . Beautiful, thanks a lot . . . now, I can continue . . . okay, who do we have now?

Betty, twenty-one, works as a key-punch operator in a sporting goods company. A graduate of Roosevelt High School, a brunette with brown eyes, she loves all kinds of music, and roller-skating. She likes watching Lawrence Welk on TV and her favorite singer at the moment is Bobby Vinton. She gives Ed a kiss, too, and then hangs up.

At three thirty Ed moves out of his swivel chair for the first time all night, giving the microphone over to Stan Freberg's comic routine about listening to the radio, and about early radio heroes. While it's playing, Ed hears from the control room that there is no security guard on the downstairs door. In a few moments the guard is located, drowsing in a room off the lobby. Ed is momentarily furious, but his anger peaks and vanishes in a matter of seconds. Totally efficient himself, he reacts strongly to sloppiness or inefficiency in others, frowning if a record is begun a split second too late or a news spot interjected too early.

Next, Mildred from the North Side calls in to ask Ed what his hobbies are, what he likes to eat, reversing the program's format and giving him temporary, but only temporary, pause. . . . *Mildred, dear, my favorite hobbies are answering phones and reading three or four books a week; and for me love is second to Chinese food; now, what about you?*

Reading is a hobby of mine, too, Ed, and I love traveling. I'm forty-five, five foot three, brown-eyed, and my hair is brown with a tiny bit of grey in it. I've got a good figure . . . yes I do, too . . . and people say I've got very good legs. She laughs, enjoying her own audacity. And I'm interested in men who don't drink or smoke, and who know how to treat a lady with respect.

Thank you, Mildred . . . thanks a lot.

Ed cues the control room and introduces John Denver's recording of "Late Night Radio." After late sports scores, Ed answers a call from Rosemary, age twenty-nine, in Berwyn.

Rosemary has a grudge. It is as if she is continuing an argument, rather than beginning a conversation.

Women shouldn't be treated like animals, Ed. I've been proposed to four times, if you want to know. His mother was going to disown him if he married me. . . . I'm Italian and he wasn't Catholic. I would've been marrying a baby; it wouldn't have worked out. His old mother, though; it makes me so angry to think of her. . . .

*Easy, there, Rosemary . . . calm down, dear. Is this the
same guy who proposed to you all four times?*

No, no . . . four different guys, and I said I'd
think it over. . . . As if I wasn't good enough for
him . . . anyway, I've got a lot of time left, right?
I'm not even thirty and I go out a lot. I'm not an
animal. Do you like baseball, Ed? Are you a Cub fan?
I am. I go out a lot. . . .

Tell us what you look like, Rosemary. . . .

I don't know, Ed. Sometimes it really gets to you.
. . . What do I look like? . . . I'm five five and I've
got brown hair and hazel eyes and I'm what you call
a sweater girl, I guess. . . . I'm not working right
now.

*Okay, Rosemary, maybe proposal number five is right
around the corner . . . you relax, now; we love you . . .
you take it easy . . . thanks for calling.*

The next caller is relaxed, easygoing. Rosemary's
fragmented fury is gone, back into the night, and
Willie from Zion laughs good-naturedly as she explains that she's called in before, a few weeks earlier,
but that nothing happened. Maybe this time my luck
will change, she says, and Ed agrees.

Willie works for Spiegel's catalogue and likes
sports: bowling, roller-skating, swimming. She
speaks with a lilt unlike the metre of the other
callers. Southern, but not rural. I'm five foot one
and a half, and I've got blonde hair and brown eyes;
and I go out to the movies more often than I read a
book. . . . I like comedies best, I guess. I came here
five years ago from Baltimore, on a visit to see my
brother, and I'm still here. . . . I like it here, sure.

How old should Mister Wonderful be, Willie . . . and what should he look like?

Willie says, Mister Wonderful should be from twenty-nine to somewhere short of a cadaver, and as for looks, I'm not all that choicey. . . . Just as long as he's warm and single.

Good for you, Willie; you're our last call this morning, and you're a lovely way to close out . . . that's Willie from Baltimore . . . the magic number is twenty. Thanks to all you gals calling in; now it's up to you fellas.

Another public health message about VD, followed by a UFO information tape from Dr. Huynek at Northwestern University. A song by Janis Ian follows, and then there is an ad for a Niles College production of *Hamlet*.

Abruptly, the morning's I guesses and I supposes and all the vital statistics in between are ended. Out in the night the sound of the women's voices hangs suspended in a soft grid over the white city. The men reach up as they will, grasping at detail.

The first male call comes in a few minutes before four thirty, from a twenty-one-year-old named Gary, asking to be put in touch with number seventeen, Betty, the twenty-one-year-old key-puncher. Gary has called in before and is known to Ed. He makes his living writing letters in Braille; he is blind.

The second caller asks for Suki; Ed checks him out by taking the number he's left and calling back on another line to make sure he's legitimate.

While the calls are coming in, another Johnny

Mathis record is playing. The men are not on the air; theirs are confidential conversations.

Caller number three is named Rusty, has called before, and wants to talk to Valerie, and to Donna from Darien. Ed gives out the name of the young mother with more pleasure than that of the young nurse and wishes him Godspeed. He is gruff with the men, wanting to make sure they are not going to give the women any trouble. He admonishes them to act like gentlemen, to behave themselves. He means it.

After Johnny Mathis, Ed announces a sing-along record of "Michael, Row the Boat Ashore."

Come on, all you sports out there in Palos Hills, Brighton Park, Broadview, and Evergreen. Let's hear it from Arlington Heights and Evanston, from Park Forest and Winnetka. . . . The music plays, more men call in . . . air time is getting thinner and thinner. The fourth caller asks for Betty; the fifth—a thirty-two-year-old from Aurora named John—asks for Donna and for Michelle, the mother of two.

At four forty-five Ed throws his arms up, signaling the final theme. *Thank you all for being with me tonight . . . we've talked to some good people; next week it's gentlemen only. . . . You guys can keep calling in, now . . . that's all the air time we've got . . . please, just have a good time out there.*

The men continue to call in, while on the air actor Alexander Scourby fills ten minutes with the Book of Genesis. A number of the callers are already known to Ed; they've built up some good will, and he feels he can give out the women's numbers to these with a clear conscience. With others he uses the telephone call-back ploy. Only once does he flatly refuse to give out any numbers, suggesting the caller not try again; this he does on intuition, because of something in the caller's voice. When it comes to voices, he says he always trusts his intuition.

A man named Casim Ali asks for Betty and for the slightly confused Rosemary from Berwyn. Walter, working as a night guard in a downtown bank, asks to be put in touch with Nora and with Suki. Gene, age thirty-four, wants Suki and Michelle; Bob, age thirty-five, a Sears worker, wants Suki and Donna and pleads to be given Nora's number as well. Ed demurs.

A twenty-five-year-old plumber from LaGrange asks for twenty-one-year-old Betty and forty-five-year-old Mildred. Are you sure those are the two you want? Ed asks. He is; they are.

There is a telephone queue. Ed's date-matching service occurs once every other week, with men calling in for women's numbers, or vice versa, only on the morning of the preceding interviews. They must wait on the line, for hours sometimes, to get through. Other nights on other topics, telephone attempts pass the four-figure mark. The audience is large, and so is its response. Ed sits at his table-desk and personally processes each call as it comes through.

His voice is now a shorthand version of itself; one-to-one conversations are not the same as one-to-thousands. Twenty-two-year-old Roger Burnett asks for Betty; Mike, a twenty-eight-year-old pre-med student, wants to get in touch with Nora. Jerry in Western Springs, thirty years old, an employee of General Foods, a film buff, wants Star Trek nut Pearl, and also Sharon the nurse. . . . Ralph of Wilmette wants Suki. . . . Sam from Des Plaines wants Cindy. Harry wants Valerie. Ron Smith wants Valerie. Twenty-six-year-old Robert wants twenty-six-year-old Michelle.

Age. The way the voices laugh. Even the fact that they've been married before. It's a rarefied method of attraction, focusing as it does on each voice, each shade of color and meaning, and vulnerability. Vocal courtship: the wooing of voices, by other voices, in the night.

The calls continue until six thirty. Horace from Elgin asks for Rosemary. Suitors group together unknowing. As the last calls come in, Betty emerges as the most popular; two more calls come in from the northern suburbs, each requesting her number and hers alone. None who ask for her knows others have. Three lights on the face of the telephone are left to darken. A thirty-seven-year-old claims adjuster named Randy, calling all the way from Peoria, wants Willie.

Another student calls for Betty. The last male call is for Valerie, from a widower named Henry, in Morton Grove.

The sunrise occurs at 6:51. Leaving the studio, riding down in the padded elevator, saying hello to the doorman, Ed, except for his size, seems the least prepossessing of men. He wears a ski parka and tan nondescript slacks, a sport shirt, and no hat over his dark curly hair.

The sky is still dim; and standing on the steps of the station building, Ed is in no position actually to see the sun. The air outside is cold, but it is calm. The lions of Michigan Avenue some blocks distant still have ice between their teeth. Ed moves quickly down the steps, his body maintaining the energy level of his voice.

He slides into his car, equipped with all manner of citizen's band gimmickry, and pulls out into the snow-covered avenue. He drives in silence downtown through the Loop and parks, near enough to walk across the street to the Holloway House cafeteria.

Inside, he takes a tray.

Where do all the women of the world come from? Nurses and secretaries and teachers wander through his life. Sometimes he knows how they wind up with the men they find, but most of the time, he doesn't. When they get married, he goes to their weddings.

The cafeteria is grey-lit, the food is timeless, the apotheosis of anonymity. Apple juice and tomato juice and prune juice flank grapefruits topped with cherries. Prefolded omelettes that rose long before the sun are embellished with bits of red-banded cheese and clumps of bright green parsley. Behind the counters and tubs of milk and butter, men and women in green and white stand listlessly, silently passing plates.

Ed orders three scrambled eggs, three English muffins, grapefruit juice, milk, coffee, and six link sausages. The sausages are small, grudging. Yolanda and Renda, the warders of the coffee cups and the cash register, respectively, watch him with disappointed eyes as he moves his tray along, takes his coffee, and pays. He is such a big man, Welles-big and, what, two hundred fifty—three hundred pounds? They had hoped to be treated to a really gargantuan glut, a mammoth platter piled high with eggs and bread and ham and sausage and fruit. And instead he eats like a gentleman. Instead his appetites are normal.

He moves to a table. The early morning custom is not distinguished. A man of indeterminate age slumps over his cup at the next table; the table is wet and so is he. The only customers who sit in twos are policemen; the other tables hold Hopper figures etched singly against the walls. As Ed eats, a woman of seventy, bedraggled, her life in the brown bag she carries clutched at her side, passes his table, then stops. She stares at him with cold loathing and anger, about to say something hideous and bitter.

He sits without taking any notice of her. Silent, he looks past her out across the high-domed room. The world rushes in. The woman stands so close to him, glaring down at him, unspeaking. Then suddenly she has turned and is walking away. She stops again on the sidewalk outside, to glare at a passing priest.

Inside, behind the plate glass window, among the rows of littered tables a lone busboy moves slowly, carefully, like a rat in a maze. Ed sits silent, pondering the day.

Among the Exotics

After the gates of the San Diego Zoo are closed to visitors, in the hour's time before sunset and moonrise, the human traffic thins and the sound of human voices gradually fades. Across the 128 acres of the park, the slanting rays of light before dusk pick up solitary animals and animals in small herds, sidelighting them for a few minutes with a last dramatic intensity. A female ostrich, seven feet tall—all brown-grey feathers and white neck—crouches over her three-pound egg where it lies warming in the dust. Briskly, from across the dirt yard a male approaches the nest and mounts the female where she crouches. Abruptly, the still air is filled with the sound of beating wings and thudding flesh. As the male's stiff ebony feathers cover the brown feathers of the female, clouds of dirt and dust swirl up to cover them both. The male's bright pink penis, unexpected in both size and color, enlarges and enters the female only a few inches above the egg in its nest below. The animals are so enormous, their coupling so frenzied, that the last of the humans leaving the zoo stop to stare, open-mouthed. Children forget to point or laugh, stunned, perhaps, at the image of Big Bird with a colossal erection.

A mother mentions fertilization, a father laughs self-consciously. After a moment or two it is all over; the male retracts and retreats, his pink flesh recedes into the mass of black feathers. The female, dripping, sways slightly over the nest and the untouched egg for a moment, then bobs her head and body erect. Directly, she commences to galop around the enclosure, at a distance from the male, who has also begun a galop of his own. Thus the two circle the nest, now slowing to a walk, now accelerating, as the light fades.

At dusk the din of the big cats begins. Across the park, settled into valleys, are the sections where lions, tigers, and jaguars are kept. From there the sound of their roaring moves up and across the zoo's canyons and valleys like balls of thunder, exploding and rolling across the sky. Underneath the darkening sky the big cats are moved into their night cages, some of them anxious, a few hesitant, roaring at the keepers and at each other, marking the change of light.

On the hill above the main section of the zoo, in the zoo hospital, a young Siberian male tiger, Sernur, and a young male lion, Sanetti, lie in wire cages side by side. At this time of early night there is a special tension in the two cages. Each of the animals is roughly three years old, and each has been hand-raised. They're kept apart from their parent colony, in a limbo of sorts, while they await shipment to another zoo, or the death of their sires.

Sernur rises, the dark stripes on his pale coat rippling as he moves. Siberian tigers are the largest of all the big cats, and among the rarest.

He pads a step forward and then swiftly, without a noise of any kind, throws his four-hundred-pound body against the wire, locking his claws in its mesh. The wire shakes with the impact; in the next cage Sanetti slowly turns toward the sound, then after a moment returns his gaze and his full attention to the direction of the roaring in the valley. Both animals remain tensely attentive in the gathering darkness. Though there is little for them to see in the hospital courtyard where they are caged, neither shuts his eyes until the evening has passed into quiet.

In the main aviary and primate section of the zoo, inside the high-domed open-air enclosure that houses a band of spider monkeys, one pale monkey screeches at a wandering flock of peahens and peacocks standing on the outside of the enclosure looking in. The half-dozen other monkeys swinging by their tails and wispy limbs contribute an occasional supportive bark to the pale monkey's tirade. Only after some twenty minutes, when his voice has grown nearly hoarse, does his scolding cease. The birds then continue on their way, their long tails dragging the ground, their blue necks arching. Uninterested in the cage when it is quiet, they move regally on.

The zoo's vast acreage is divided into canyons and mesas, with flat enclosures alternating with steep, tree-shrouded inclines. There are six main plateaus and a like number of valleys.

Near the main entrance, in the nursery within the children's zoo, Shannon, the nursery attendant, is rearranging the corners of a five-month-old pygmy chimpanzee's diaper. The young male ape is one of the zoo's small colony, six children of a mother born in Antwerp. KC, as the young male is called, is older by a month than the female siamang—a species of gibbon—in the crib next to him. The gibbon mother had two offspring before Holly and was unable to provide enough milk for them; she died shortly after Holly was pulled. KC bounces up and down in his crib. He is fed every one to three hours, on demand; Holly gets a mixture of milk, Enfamil, and a bit of blended cereal only once every three hours. The two young apes both have dark hair, silky to the touch; KC's is already growing in small tufts inside his ears. Slivers of white hair grow on pygmy rumps and no others, and pygmy fingers are webbed up to the second joint. Aside from these physical details, KC exhibits the behavior specialty of his tribe as well: he stands fidgeting with his fingers while Shannon rearranges his pants and then opens his mouth, keeping it wide enough to give the semblance of a questioning expression. When Shannon nods her head at him, he makes a soft chirping sound and then pushes his head back against the mattress of the crib. His mouth remains half-open, smiling, and his eyes continue to gaze up at her face.

Then, after a moment, he begins what is his nightly vocal exercise—an uninterrupted period of from forty to sixty minutes of shrieking and screaming, punctuated by those asides which comprise a pygmy's special genius. Other chimpanzees in captivity may resort to one or the other of two vocal attitudes when they open their mouths, either a stream of frustrated screams or a low babble. KC's performance ranges up and down, from treble to bass and back again. The screaming will subside in a few months' time, as has happened with his older sister. As he matures his pattern will become quieter, more conversational.

Shannon moves to the other end of the nursery to check on the animals' formula where it heats on a hot plate next to the double sink. The room is twenty-four by fifteen feet, or about four crib lengths long. KC's crib is a white Winnie the Pooh affair, with a brown teddy bear and a rubber duck on the mattress. Holly's crib is smaller, less decorated. She lies in her crib quietly, a tenuous bundle of dark hair and flesh, her eyes following Shannon's movements about the room. At the far end of the nursery are two upright cages that house KC's older sister, Loretta Lynn, and a five-month-old hanuman langur named Tommy. When KC begins his screaming, Tommy picks up his own complaint, chattering in midair as he leaps back and forth behind the wire. Shannon tests the formula, then brings it over to Holly and begins feeding her. Holly closes her eyes as she sucks the rubber nipple; after the bottle is half-finished, Shannon replaces her in her crib; despite the noise of KC and Tommy, she is soon asleep.

Outside in the darkening light, the evening air around the nursery takes on the heavy odor of oranges and plumeria. The scent of the trees hangs in the air, blending with the animal and paddock smells, with the autumnal smell of apples and oranges in the open kitchen, with the sweetish smell of Enfamil and fresh milk in the nursery.

In the tall trees beside the flamingo pond, a group of peacocks moves upward through the green limbs, spreading their tail feathers as they settle, each on a separate bough. In the dusky light the iridescent eyes of their blue-green tails peer out like small lanterns from among the leaves. They are silent once they have settled on their perches; below them the flamingos stand like heavy pink flowers on their single legs, unmoving, heads buried in the feathers of their spines. From time to time a bird raises its head and calls out, its voice the sound of a bicycle horn, and is answered by another voice from across the pond. Their crooked necks are brilliant stalks among the drab foliage of the small guinea fowl who peck at the grass around the lagoon. Nearer the water's edge, the fowls' fat domino-spotted bodies bob slowly, complacently.

A pair of roseate spoonbills now appear at the water's edge. First one then the other scoops at the still water, dipping its head to drink.

Among the standing flamingos a black swan moves slowly through the water. Declining to emerge where the guinea fowl graze, instead it spreads its inky feathers on the shore at the far end of the lagoon. There it stands, preening its tail feathers, after every few passes of its beak wagging its clump of feathers in the manner of a spaniel wagging its tail.

The darkness gathers around it where it stands, and after a time its outline disappears.

Farther down, some distance from the pond, in the enormous screened aviary the sound of fluttering wings blends with the rush of running water, the small waterfalls and fountains slowing for the night. Golden pheasants scurry about in the underbrush, while above them Indian black ibises and white ibises look down from the cypresses, their scimitar beaks curving obliquely toward the earth. Already invisible are softly squawking parrots, grey and inconspicuous against the leaves. The smell is of mulch and dew.

A black-breasted Himalayan monal shakes its turquoise-green crest and then swoops down to the edge of a waterfall pool. The sharp odor of fish hangs over the water; herons and egrets with heads lowered beneath its surface move tentatively, a step at a time, along the shore edge. A mallard pecks at a dead minnow and then moves on to browse among snails and leaves in a small eddy. A crimson-rumped toucanet swoops through the air above the waterfall and thuds gently to the ground.

Behind all these sounds there is the fragile trilling and cooing of small parakeets, their notes like soft bubbles of hot glass.

In the snake house the eye of a Pope's tree viper looks out from behind its glass-walled cage. The eye is pale and milky, elliptical pupil and yellow iris clouded over, preparatory to the shedding of the body's skin. The viper, some three feet long, lies with its pale green underside draped across a plastic tree and moves slowly against its stiff leaves; the large triangular head is held erect as its red-brown tail twitches against the glass.

The viper is nocturnal, unlike other snakes in the enclosure. The scales move slowly against the brittle leaves, and the process of shedding is gradually and systematically begun.

Shannon makes her cleaning and feeding rounds every two hours in the nursery. The young animals in the paddock outside and behind the main nursery building are on a normal nursing routine, not varying a great deal from the bihourly schedule inside. In addition to Holly, KC and Loretta Lynn, and Tommy, there is also a wallaby of one and a half years who lives in the nursery and who is given eight ounces of canned milk and water every morning, along with a large bowl of vegetables and alfalfa.

There are usually between twenty-five and thirty babies cared for during every twelve-month span in the zoo nursery. They are brought in because of sickness or injuries, or because they have been orphaned, or because they have some congenital defect. Francis, the wallaby, has such a defect: a pair of bad kidneys that require large amounts of citrus. He follows Shannon about the room, moving quietly, like the shadow of a yo-yo on a wall.

Between the nursery and the paddock is a back nursery, a narrow room lined with the cages of small primates and quadrupeds, and one rather testy owl named Barney. The first stall holds a Grant's gazelle with a broken leg. As Shannon strokes the animal along the spine, its ears move back and forth like thin radar screens. Next to the gazelle is a bush dog that has been brought over from Germany to mate; it circles in its cage, making a steady whining sound.

It stops for a moment as she passes, then resumes. A young kinkajou, his coat a brownish gold, stares out from behind the mesh, pushing his nose against her palm. What appears to be half-rat, half-rabbit sits on short paws with its long black tail curled beneath it: a springhaas from South Africa, brought over, like the bush dog, to mate in California. In the cage adjoining the springhaas are three proper rabbits, large black Netherlander bucks. They too are there to breed.

The barn owl in his cage creates a screeching havoc when Shannon passes the cage next to his containing a dozen baby chicks; they, along with ground horse meat, are all he ever eats.

Shannon moves slowly, efficiently, among the animals. She wears a gold smock and blue jeans; her dark hair falls lightly forward, framing her face as she peers into one after the other of the long line of cages. Barney ceases his screeching and the agitated beating of his wings after she passes by the chickens' cage. She begins feeding the young gazelle a bottle of milk, half goat's milk and half kitten's milk. For the gazelle's broken bone to mend, it needs a great deal of protein and calcium: four ounces of the formula every two hours.

A pair of wallabies has earlier been brought into the back nursery to mate; the female lies contentedly on her bed of hay while the male hops about, sniffing at the wire of the cage, his pink tongue flicking up and across his damaged nose and lip. Female wallabies are often more aggressive than other marsupials, and another female of the colony has at some point bitten off most of the male's upper lip.

Shannon passes the wallabies, crossing to where a
desert fox named Sonora pads quietly to the door of
its cage to be scratched behind the ears. Sonora has
been hand-raised and has never run wild; she moves
about with good-natured docility. Even with animals
that have been hand-raised, this docility sometimes
undergoes a change once they have mated and bred
offspring of their own. Parenthood makes them
slightly more squeamish about human contact.
Shannon scratches her soft fur and, as she does, Sonora wags her tail appreciatively. Foxes and wolves
show pleasure in much the same manner as their domestic relations; after a few moments of being petted
and scratched, Sonora pads back to the window side
of her cage and after a short circling movement re-
settles into the straw.

Shannon seems at perfect ease as she makes her
rounds; she is twenty-two, a woman who has grown
up with animals and who accepts them as they accept
her, matter-of-factly. She lives in San Diego with her
aunt and uncle and takes classes during the day. At
San Diego State her field of study is animal husbandry, and her special interest is exotic medicine,
the care and treatment of zoo animals. Veterinary
medicine that concerns horses, pigs, cattle, or domestic dogs and cats is considered nonexotic; Shannon for her part feels she is best suited for work
among the exotics. She prefers working at night,
when there are fewer distractions and, especially
during the summer months, fewer faces peering in
at the nursery through its glass wall. She comes to
work a half-hour before the day attendant leaves,

learning from her the details of any new births, or any new formulas.

On the blackboard in the kitchen room where apples and oranges are stacked on a long table, next to the nursery, there is a message concerning the activity in the paddock during the day just passed. A mouflon sheep has lost her baby because of internal complications during birth; the message from the day attendant records the birth, the lamb's death, and the nature of the afterbirth. Another notation prescribes a mixture of canned milk and water, twenty-four ounces of which are to be given to a young black yak, also in the paddock, every four hours. There is also a brief note saying that Tommy the langur has refused milk twice during the day.

She takes the empty bottle from the gazelle and makes one last round of the cages, stopping for a moment in front of an ancient saki, a small New World monkey whose thick coat of hair has grown silver with age. The saki, a female of twenty-five years, has outlived all her familial colony and now concentrates her energy on climbing up onto a single wooden branch each day. She awakens as Shannon, her junior by three years, freshens the water at the cage door. The eyelids of the smaller primate remain at half-mast as she slowly moves her head toward the sound of splashing liquid. After identifying the sound, she resumes her attitude of sleep. Of the primates, she is the oldest in the back nursery, and the quietest.

Back in the main nursery, KC is bouncing in his

crib and his sister at her end of the room is making a
series of hooting calls, seemingly directed at the television set beside the entrance door. As Shannon returns to the room, she switches channels, and immediately both KC and his sister quiet down. They
complain whenever the screen switches from color to
black and white, and they prefer game shows to football or other sports events. What they really like
most are the soap operas; they talk to themselves
and to each other, filling in the pauses, listening and
explaining themselves until they grow tired.

At moonrise, across the park, the lemurs join
together in a barking chorus. The red-ruffed lemurs
tend to assert their authority over the ring-tailed
lemurs and are kept apart from them. Though they
are separated by cages of macaques and howler
monkeys, they communicate by screaming and braying at each other, reminding themselves of their
levels of hierarchy. Suddenly, a large red-ruffed
male begins a series of alarm screeches, head lowered toward the earth, black hands and feet tensely
gripping the branches of his bough. In their cages,
together and apart, all the lemurs take up the new
cry. Soon all heads arch downward, like those of the
water birds of the lagoon, as the colony alerts itself
to the change of light and the change of shadows on
the ground. In the wild, on an island like Nosy
Mangabe off Madagascar, the change in light sig-
nifies a change of activity and mood. The life of nocturnal lemurs is marked by a cyclical drop in body
temperature during the day, and therefore the first
minutes of the evening are spent warming up to the

pace of the night. The aye-aye, one of the rarer lemurs, emerges from its nest in the wild, tentatively,
cautiously, moving at the pace of its metabolism as it
slowly gathers momentum.

An aye-aye amid the chorus of lemurial braying—
a racket that resembles as much the amplified crow-
ing of roosters as it does the screeching of the other
primates—moves slowly along his own shadowy
branch, ears swiveling in the darkness. With ears
that are large and membranous, he picks up the
smaller sounds beneath the larger din. His hearing is
so acute that he is able to hear even the faint
scratches of beetle larvae inside rotten wood.

In the reptile house, the tree viper continues its
process of shedding. It moves imperceptibly against
the green plastic leaves, its thin skin, like bits of
spider webbing, hanging in soft shards from its
body. Next to it in a cage of its own, a Mexican pit
viper, head erect and bobbing, watches over its
young, three tiny brown strips of flesh with light
green tail tips. The Mexican female's mature body is
ebony, dotted with milky green; she tests the air
again and again with her long forked tongue.

The evening security guard, a retired Army man
named Angelo, flashes his light across the glass cages as
he passes on his rounds. The reflection of the flash-
light on the glass creates a counterfeit moon for an
instant in the viper's small universe, and is then extinguished. The light moves on, in a series of short
exposures, following the rounded curve of the reptile house.

Angelo moves across the grass, the light moving in jagged flashes as he walks onward, away from the snakes, toward the Nocturnal Canyon.

Shannon crouches over the bed of hay in which Francis the wallaby spends his nights. When he sleeps, he tucks and folds his body as if he were still inside his mother's pouch, curling up with his tail around him. His bed of hay is changed two or three times a night, depending on how dirty he's made it. Like apes and humans, wallabies are fascinated by their own waste, composing elaborate finger paintings with it on the floor. The most fastidious of animal babies are the big cats; neither lions, jaguars, nor tigers are at all interested in this area of their own biology.

When there are baby cats in the nursery, there is considerably more activity. Francis the wallaby and Loretta Lynn the chimp continually chase each other about, and Loretta Lynn climbs on the back of any four-footed vehicle that passes. She is especially partial to young aardvarks and tigers. Most cats stay in the nursery only until their third or fourth month and then are moved back into regular zoo quarters or, like Sernur and Sanetti, relegated to the hospital courtyard to await placement elsewhere.

There is a great variety of animal habit. In the nursery, as across the park, cats and dogs and other carnivores are more active at night than the majority of animals. There are nocturnal prosimians and diurnal quadrupeds, and animals such as the hippopotamus, whose days are spent in brown water up to the lidded eyeballs, but whose nights in the wild are passed on land, grazing. The change of element is with the hippopotamus crucial to its societal behavior; shoulder to shoulder and tail to tail in the mud, there are few territorial quibbles. But on land distances must be maintained, and the benign tolerance of the day gives way to much competitive tussling and rutting.

After sundown, in their enclosure, the zoo's colony of koalas make their ambling way down to a central pile of eucalyptus leaves, on which they commence to feed. The animals drink little, if any, water, instead drawing much of the moisture their systems absorb from the sickle-shaped leaves. The small marsupials chew patiently, methodically, muzzles wrinkling and unwrinkling as they go through the pile. There are a number of eucalyptus groves in the park, with some trees reaching up to a height of seventy-five feet. They group together in tall stands, overlooking blinking Chinese leopards in their cages.

Clouded leopards pace slowly under banks of silk oak and fuchsia as the full moon rises. At the end of the park, in the wolf enclosure, a mother suckles her young by its pale light. The young wolves are a week old, and there are four of them, wet and black and hungry. In this first week, while they are suckling, their grey mother's eyes seldom close. Now she yawns, tensing the skin of her neck and brow, and bends to lick the nearest furry head.

Farther down in the canyon, hyenas and dingoes, all nocturnal hunters, raise their own salutatory cry.

The hyena's harsh gasp, like a plea of the deranged, crosses the grassy canyon. The pack of dogs lies pressed together in the dust, the many-throated howl coming from it as if from one single animal. Beside the pathway, the cream-white blossom of a night-scented butterfly-orchid lies unmoving, with its petals spread. Its scent blends into the chorus of animal cries. In the moonlit night the white blossom will shine upward through the darkness, luring down and into its deep spurs moths of long and slender proboscis. Pollination at night is carried out by flower species that rely on scent rather than color to attract moths and hummingbirds. Variegated orchids which grow outside the park rely on other mechanisms to attract their pollinators. There, a number of terrestrial orchids carry flowers that look very much like those insects they wish to attract. The blossoms so resemble the females of certain species of fly, bumblebee, or spider that the male is attracted to the blossoms as to a mate. The blossoming of these orchids, called fetish orchids, is timed so that they are in full bloom at a time when the male insects are flying about but the females have not yet emerged in their adult procreative state. Such masquerading has its effect, and a number of males do come to rest on the fetish blossoms and so carry away their pollen. Still, the method is not foolproof, relying as it does on masculine whim, and many of these orchids have a safeguard means of self-pollination as well.

Moth flowers open at night. Their pale flowers, too, attract nocturnal pollinators by the intensity of their odor rather than by color. A hawk moth hovers over an evening primrose for only a moment, beating the air with its wings while it feeds, its body brushing against the blossom's anthers and stigma. Its proboscis retracted, directly it moves on to a single lily and, after a moment, to a patch of tuberoses, whose heady aroma floats in the night air like a warm liquid current.

Officially, there are no bats within the confines of the zoo. Yet they do pass through, and their erratic flight through the night air is an arresting sight. Inactive by day, after sundown they leave caves and tree roosts to swoop out across the desert, their flight describing a pattern of hexagrams and rhomboids, unlike the ovals and circles of the night birds' flight. Bats are color-blind and rely on their sense of smell rather than sight to distinguish plants whose flowers will provide nectar.

Across the mountains and the desert, against the moon, a dozen bats are silhouetted as they touch down at a giant saguaro cactus. The bats hover at each blossom for only a moment, their slender black tongues uncoiling and coiling over the thick nectar. The fur of their faces and wings picks up bits of pollen released by their movement. As they fly in one body on to the next cactus spire, the layer of residue appears nearly phosphorescent beneath the moon.

Back inside the park, in the ostrich enclosure, the male has taken over from the female at the nest and now sits with folded legs and wings atop the three-pound egg. His long neck is arched slightly as from time to time he twists his head in response to the various night sounds around him. He has the largest eye of any terrestrial creature, winged or unwinged, and his vision is acute at great distances. The female at the far end of the enclosure stands motionless on her enormous cloven feet, the new egg within her, fertilized at dusk, proceeding in its growth pattern until, in three days' time, it too will drop into the body-warmed nest. The smaller birds in their aviaries call to one another across the foliage, but the pair of ostriches is silent throughout the night. On the nest the male shifts his weight and blinks at the moon.

A South American uakari, a short-nosed monkey with a bright pink face, scampers back and forth beneath the heat lamp which is attached to the ceiling of his open-air cage. Against the night, and with the heat warming his features, his face appears almost scarlet. He chatters a low monologue, moving close to and then farther away from the comfort of the familiar heat.

Not far from the koalas' colony is the brightly lit kiwi house, halfway down a sloping pathway, cut off from natural light and natural temperature changes. Inside, the flightless birds are asleep. During daylight hours the glass-fronted enclosure inside is dimly lit, simulating moonlight. In New Zealand these rare birds are active only at night, and the zoo has effectively changed their environment so that San Diego day passes for Auckland night. Automatic timing devices control dimmers so that counterfeit

dusk falls and dawn comes up, gradually, at the pace
of natural habit. These counterfeit days lengthen in
summer and shorten in winter; the seasonal alteration of day length is believed to affect the birds'
nervous and endocrine systems. Zoo-bred birds
adapt better and more quickly to this alteration of
natural pattern; first-generation birds, however,
such as those who now lie sleeping, hairlike feathers
spread against the leaves, may still dream of true
night and true day. True night is their home, their
genetic territory, and although they accommodate
their physical surroundings, they are perhaps not, in
the most thorough sense of the word, adapted to
them. Merely resting in the false day, their sleep is
as much a counterfeit as the false light that appears
to induce it.

In their glass enclosure, another colony of flightless birds, the penguins, goes about its watery business undaunted by moonlight. In the penguin house
a dozen birds stand together on a raised platform,
taking turns beneath the spray of the raised showers.
They move in caricature, performing as any group
of portly gentlemen might at a Turkish bath, gab-
bling to each other in voices that evoke the worn-out
honks of a New Year's Eve noisemaker. Others dive
down into a green-water pool, yellow-breasted King
penguins and lesser penguins alike, feet thrust like
rudders behind them, black wings spread. From underneath they look like bulky jet planes, and their
passage seems as swift and smooth through the
green-lit water.

All across the park those animals whose activities
are largely diurnal are bedded down for the night,
usually in pairs. Two parchment-eared elephants,
the zoo's largest, are allowed to remain out in the air
while the remainder of the herd is being moved inside
the pachyderm house. The rhinos are kept in separate stalls, as are the okapis, elsewhere. Fenced off
from one another by day as well as night, the two African okapis twitch black flesh on flanks slashed with
white stripes as they stand napping primly. Black
tongues and white teeth relaxed from their constant
chewing for a few hours, they sleep against the trees.

The larger elephant is not asleep; with her ancient
eye she stands regarding the moon. The long grey
trunk descends to the dirt and then, raising a small
cloud of dust, searches idly along the fence line for a
bit of peanut shell, a mint. Finding none, it curls
upward, the stiff hairs at its tip focusing for the moment only on the cool night air.

Two Bactrian camels are kept together at night,
their shaggy golden bodies side by side. In the darkness their humps appear to wear toupees; when the
bodies move with the lurching, mincing motion
which is all their own, the humps rock slightly, the
mats of hair bobbing back and forth, up and down.
Now they kneel to earth, settling into their pattern
of sleep, lowering their long necks slowly, inch by
inch, until they too lie motionless in the dust.

The watch has changed, and Angelo, the pa-
trolling security guard, has given over his duty to
Dina, a red-haired woman in her thirties. Dina has
been on the job only a matter of months, making her

night rounds of the animals much as her husband
outside the zoo makes his, installing and servicing
burglar alarms in the San Diego suburbs.

Dina rides over the same course as Angelo has earlier, checking the locks on all the enclosures, making
sure there are no disturbances in the various pens. She
drives past the night sentinel upon whom both she
and Angelo have come to rely, an African crowned
crane that stands on a small rise beside the roadway.
It silently blinks in the wash of light from the patrol
car's headlamps. The crane is a constant in the
changing zoo night; if one night it were not to appear, or if it were in some way agitated, the pa-
trolling guard would know something was out of balance in the park's scheme of things. Such imbalance
is rare; Dina believes that the zoo at night is a privi-
leged place, a sort of religious sanctuary, a church.
In zoos there are periodic reports of animals slain
and of their young being stolen; Marwell Zoo outside London has a number of eggs stolen from beneath nesting Manchurian cranes; in New York's
Central Park the zoo is forced to build higher fences
after deer are slaughtered in the night. But in San
Diego security is tight and thorough. One incident in
recent history has been the theft of a cheetah cub; although such an incident is extremely rare, it cannot
be ignored. And so the locks are checked with increased frequency, and the animals inspected and
counted even more meticulously than before.

Dina passes a field of zebras, asleep where they
stand, their striped bodies like clumps of grounded
lightning. Beyond them are standing burros and
kneeling bison, ringed by tufts of Natal plum. She

approaches the cage of a cougar named Cody, a favorite, who wheezes out a greeting as she stops the
car. The sound of the cougar is that of a doll's chest
being pressed; it is a scratchy clearing of the throat,
an irritated but affectionate acknowledgment of
Dina's presence.

After a few moments of conversation she drives
on.

In the paddock, behind the rear nursery, where
the hoofed stock is kept, Shannon unlocks a wooden
door and enters the long open corridor between two
rows of stalls. In the third stall down, a white ewe and
her two lambs nibble at the hay. Next to them a
mouflon mother and her lamb lie quietly together,
neither of them making much of Shannon's presence.
It is this mother sheep who lost a second lamb the
night before, and whose details of birth are written
inside on the board. Over the length of the paddock
are heat lamps which cast a red glow up onto the
aluminum roof; the effect is peculiar, subterranean.
Other stalls, beyond those of the sheep, house yak
offspring. The names are constantly changing: Cognac, Pontiac, and, lately, Nymphomaniac. Shannon
dispenses their mixture of canned milk and water,
giving special attention to the youngest, making sure
he gets his share, that he is able to drink it without
difficulty. There are five stalls on either side of the
paddock, and they are all filled with hoofed stock. In
the end stall a young blue-grey nilgai buck stands
with his nose raised up over the level of the stall
door. It expands and contracts slowly, amicable,
shiny and black.

Outside the paddock Shannon stops to straighten two wooden boxes which serve as living quarters for two echidna, or spiny anteaters. The entrance opening has been somehow turned against the wall of their enclosure so that the small spiny animals have been unable to enter it for the night. After checking to make sure there are no foreign animals inside, she rights it and urges them inside.

Back inside the nursery, she sweeps up the soiled hay around Francis the wallaby's nest and puts out fresh hay. The bihourly feeding and cleaning divides the night into watches for her; when the last of these is nearly finished, she checks on her primate charges to make sure they are all settled in before she leaves them alone for the few hours before dawn.

Loretta Lynn lies in her cage quietly sucking on her thumb as she watches Shannon sweep up the hay. KC pulls himself erect and bounces for a few minutes in his crib, then gives all his attention to his reflection in a mirror beside the crib. Shannon says primates, generally, are stimulated by their own reflections and enjoy altering their appearance in the mirror by piling on bits of clothing and whatever other props are at hand. KC reaches out and very gently touches his own face in the glass, and after one more perfunctory bounce lies down, resuming his attitude of sleep.

Sleep needs vary from animal to animal, from species to species. Most four-footed stock, such as the animals of the paddock and other domestic breeds of cattle, sheep, and goats, are thought to require no more than three or four hours for every twenty-four-hour period. In the field these grazing animals spend the best part of their activity ingesting their food supply, a task that uses up both their time and energy. Contrasted with the grazing herbivores are animals who need only a few hours in which to gather their food, mammals such as the opossum and the armadillo. These are active for only as many hours as the sheep and cattle are inactive; compared with the browsers and grazers, they spend their lives in patterns of relative leisure and ease. In a third category are animals that are thought to require no sleep at all, such as the porpoise and the tree shrew. Hoofed stock are prey to carnivores when their eyes are closed, whereas a creature such as the armadillo is protected from predators by his hard shell as much while sleeping as while awake. All young animals, as a rule, need more sleep than adults, and in the nursery the infant apes sleep for longer periods than do their elders out in the ape compound. The higher primates as a group are diurnal in their habits, with the activity of most monkeys and apes beginning just before dawn and continuing, through a midday pause, on toward sunset.

The owl monkey of South America is the single exception to this primate rule and does his feeding at night. (There are 140 known species of monkeys and apes, and the owl monkey, or douroucouli, is the only one of these whose habits are exclusively nocturnal. The owl monkey, when young, is kept in its mother's nest, usually in a dark hole in a tree, and is trained to follow its parents' pattern of feeding and sleeping. It is the only species of monkey that constructs a nest to sleep in, making it even more singular.)

In the woodlands of Africa, apes, however, do construct nests around them in which they spend the night. In their California enclosures the impulse toward night nest-building stays with them, and in the ape compound a large gorilla named Albert goes through a brief ritual in gorilla shorthand, pushing a few twigs and leaves together to simulate a mountain nest as night approaches. Albert is twenty-four, a full-bodied primate whose dark eyes and creased forehead appear to be focused in continuing judgment of those who pass before him. The cells of his cerebral cortex are remarkably active; he holds grudges for years and is known for his antipathy toward certain keepers. Before dusk and in the early morning hours, his ritual includes a stealthy circumlocution of the enclosure's moat, a quiet approach toward his keeper, hands held discreetly behind ebony brown back, now silvered with age. At a certain point the hands suddenly appear, to hurl quantities of feces at that zoo keeper against whom his grudge is nursed. It is a brief display, and after his point is made, he retires to the less hostile activity of his days. Now he dozes, palm open on the cement, his massive frame expanding and contracting with the effort of sleep.

In the high-vaulted orangutan section a hundred feet distant from Albert, before entering her sleeping quarters, an adolescent female ambles across the concrete, her orange-grey face round and benign as the moon above her. Grey flesh and henna hair are in dark contrast to the pale pink of her palms and the soles of her feet. Reaching a spot near the glass which gives off the gorilla section, she sprawls gracefully on the ground, rolling slowly first one way, then the other, on her back. Her eyes are soft, with long fine lashes and pale lids; in the gathering darkness they are kind, intuitive, expressive. Her ears are small, like soft brown snails, and her great puffed upper lip is lined with numberless thin creases. As she lies on her back she lifts one long arm above her, letting rivulets of cool dirt fall from between her fingers down onto her neck and shoulders. She slowly scoops up more dirt and with both hands plays with its fall along her neck, down across the length of her body and back against her cheeks and across her forehead. She thrusts her legs upward, hands that are feet and feet that are hands tickling the air. When her hands are empty, her toes fold in upon themselves, and she lowers her arms to the ground on either side. Her right hand finds a bit of grass and she pulls it to her mouth, first tracing it across her lips, then chewing slowly, experimentally. Her fingernails are black against her face. After a long pause she again spreads her arms out on either side, hands gently opening and closing as she lies on her back, her eyes gazing upward at the moon, soft and smiling.

On the side of a rocky slope, beyond the wolves, a herd of African gazelles flashes across the beam of Dina's light. Their white tails blaze up and disappear in the darkness like bits of haiku.

A circle of deer, quivering and poised for flight, group together like a ring of mushrooms in the night's shade. Their antlers are young and tender, curling upward like soft tendrils of a sensitive forest plant. The antlers move as if in a breeze, bending and swaying, and then disappearing in the darkness as heads are lowered to the earth.

As Shannon closes the nursery door, from across the park there is a muffled bark of sea lions, a random complaint that soon fades. She leaves the zoo through the revolving aluminum gate beside the main entrance, after first double-checking the paddock and nursery outer locks. When she gets home she will sleep for four hours, then get up to drive to her animal husbandry classes that day.

In an hour the big cats will resume their roar, and the other sleeping animals will join in. The zoo's food preparers arrive at five thirty, the gardeners a half-hour later. The carnivores receive only one meal a day, in the morning. Angelo and Dina say that the morning meal time is the most difficult time for the keepers; the security officers on A.M. duty have to stay in close communication with the keepers who handle the dangerous strings, the chain of cages which include the cats, bears, and tapirs.

Now the cats are quiet and, the sound of the sea lions having faded, the zoo's enormous expanse is, for the moment, still.

Back in the Nocturnal Canyon, amid the quiet, there remains one focus of night activity. Soundlessly, in their cage, a pair of Arctic foxes, their coats darkening from winter white, take turns racing the night inside a circular wire wheel. The soundless treadmill revolves, then slackens as the first of the pair steps off, to accelerate again as the second animal immediately steps in. So they continue, running together beneath the moon, until the sky lightens above them, and the night passes.

Baby Powder

The country and suburbs of Milwaukee slope west from the Lake in a pattern of small hills and valleys. The contours of the land, shaped by the spurs of glaciers, now hold fields of agriculture and bowls of industry. Suburban homes alternate with patches of farmland. On Highway 38 south of the city a flock of grey and blue geese flies across the garage door mural of a bright pink house. Nearby, a Mexican peasant carved in concrete stands next to a concrete burro on a patch of brownish lawn. Farther south, chickens scratch and women throw out feed from aluminum pails in backyards and barnyards, in wire-enclosed roosts and pens. In the industrial Menomonee Valley, small and large factories clump together under an industrial haze of blue. The smell of the farmlands beyond is covered by that of sulfur and oil and wax. In the valley at night, bread is baked and yeast ferments; paste wax is heated and cooled, and massive ingots are transferred red-hot from steam bath to moving tray. There is a film over the valley at night, punctuated by the diesel stacks of trucks bringing in raw materials.

The men and women who work in the factories come from Illinois and Ohio and Michigan, and they come from the surrounding farmland as well. The graveyard shift in most plants is only a security shift. A plant in full-time production generally employs one-third the daytime number of working men and women at night. The majority of the workers in the Menomonee Valley who work at night in these plants are moonlighting, working two jobs at once. Ben is the exception in that his work as night foreman in a packaging plant is his only job. He makes somewhere around $275 a week.

It is a half-hour drive in Ben's Fiat from north Milwaukee to the factory. He swings down along the Lake and then across the bridge. There are still old trolley tracks in the city of Milwaukee, and he slows down for one, plugging in the tape deck and listening to Simon and Garfunkel, Stevie Wonder.

He has gotten up early enough to spend the afternoon with his younger sister and her sons. It is the youngest of these, Samuel's, birthday, and Ben has brought him an enormous stuffed serpent doll with large white felt eyelashes and brown plush spots. The child dragged it off with him across the grass and began to talk to it within an hour's time, so Ben considers the gift a success.

He pulls the car into the factory parking lot, dimming his lights at the gate.

There is a sign on Ben's front door:

DAY SLEEPER

It is made of cardboard, edged in grey, and stuck up with adhesive. The print is large and black. How

many Jehovah's Witnesses or magazine salesmen it
has kept from ringing the bell he doesn't know, but
he thinks it does some good. He also thinks it may
keep away prowlers. The house in which he has an
apartment is large and solid, in a row of other solid
houses. It is a neighborhood on the northeast side of
town in which there is little activity on the streets
during the day, and he is able to sleep from three
thirty or four in the morning until noon.

Ben's time card is always punched a few minutes
early. He arrives at work in time to check the day's
production figures and delivery notations before
going out onto the plant floor. Officially, his working
hours are from four to midnight. He enters the factory through the side door and goes directly to the
employees' locker room.

Ben is a big cartoon figure of a man. The men on
the line call him Bluto, because of his size, because of
his tattoos. On the left bicep there is the figure of a
small blue and red dragon. On the underside of his
right arm, underneath, between the tricep and bicep
muscles, are his two initials, B.A. He is six two and
has a thick black moustache.

He changes into his work clothes in the locker
room, stepping into the tan slacks and shirt and
white duckbilled cap that the company provides. He
checks his appearance in the mirror next to the large
circular sink, snaps his locker shut, and goes out
onto the floor.

Talc comes into the factory to be compressed and
processed into baby powder. It leaves a film in the
air; it is a soft greyish white material, a mineral also
used in tubes of paint and in chemical lubricants.
In the factory office Ben dusts a bit off his trou-

sers, checking against a trucker's list the amount of
soft white powder that has been delivered that day.
Talc arrives at the factory in fifty-pound bags.
The sound from two machines processing shampoo
packets echoes against the concrete floor. There is a
whoosh and a hammering, interspersed oddly with
the same sound from the machine next to it on the
line. The first machine operates at a slightly faster
rate than the second, and there is first a syncopation,
then harmony, then a counterpoint, and again syncopation, every minute and a half. The men and
women working the label line hear it with varying
degrees of attention. There are a dozen workers
running different products through the packing
lines. The factory is half-lit at night.

Ben shifts the board he is carrying and crosses to
the truck ramp to help unload some cartons. He
signs the invoices and tells the driver where to stack
them. The air at the truck entrance is thick; from inside the smell of steam and ozone spills out to com-
bine with that of motor oil and carbon monoxide.

Ben moves back into the plant, and the truck pulls
away from the loading dock. The driver moves out
onto the main road, heading back to the quarries
north of Zion. Truckers' radios crackle in rough
wrinkled voices on the Interstate; the trucks rumble
north and south, and inland from the Lake. A cloud
of grey hangs over the black valley, tinted alternately
orange and blue; a small refinery half a mile away
has as its emblem a white star, and over the main
building there is a large five-pointed star of white
electric light, which now takes color from the haze.

Women in the truck stops and the Howard Johnsons mop the counters and chew gum and look for lawyers among the drivers who stop to drink coffee. Conversation in the Valley and at the truck stops, depending on the season, is of the Bucks and the Brewers and the Green Bay Packers. Portable radios next to cash registers and truck-stop sinks broadcast Gladys Knight, the Beatles, Aretha Franklin.

Ben has been working at Downing Packaging for seven years. He switched over to nights, after working at other factories in the area at a variety of day jobs.

Point to anything in the plant and Ben will describe its function. He says it's because he's a Gemini and his sign gives him an eye for detail. He explains the workings of the baby powder machine, saying that one formula is pretty much the same as another, and that the only difference in the end product is in its packaging. Most nights, they don't run the powder line, but there is a large order from one of the supermarket chains tonight that needs filling, and so the machine is still processing the day order.

As Ben is running his hand over the surface of the compressor, a young woman comes over to where he is standing. She works on the label line and her name is Margaret.

"I brought in a chicken from one of my spider plants," she says, handing him a green and white clump of leaves in a terra-cotta pot. "I thought maybe I could trade it for some of that Swedish ivy you said you've got." She stands waiting for his answer, a young mother of two, twenty-six years old. Her face is lightly freckled, and there are strands of reddish hair curling out from under her factory cap. Ben thanks her for the spider and tells her that he'll make a point of bringing in a pot of ivy on Monday. He takes the plant from her, examining the leaves as he does, smiling.

Margaret is new on the line and has only lately come back into the working force of the Valley. She and her husband of five years have recently separated, by mutual consent, and her two sons are in school during the day while her mother in South Milwaukee takes care of them at night. She sees less of her family than she would like but is making more money working nights.

Ben takes the pot across the floor to the office, stopping on the way to check the shampoo packets on the label line. Margaret wonders to herself what the living room looks like toward which her spider is bound. She sits next to her press, sipping a cup of tea from her thermos, watching Ben as he argues with an old man named Ed about his rate of production.

Ben moves from machine to machine, and then to the loading dock, quickly, efficiently. He stops to drink from a plastic cup of coffee after an hour and a half, but then resumes his work almost immediately. He says he likes the hustle and bustle of production and prefers as many of the plant's machines to be in operation as possible. Too much of the same routine makes him feel claustrophobic, he says; he likes being able to move at right angles to himself, he likes being surprised. After his coffee he spends a

half-hour trying to find out what's wrong on one of
the conveyor belts. He finally locates the problem
and calls the machinist. He watches the process of
production through the plate glass windows of the
office and feels the satisfaction of seeing things
under control.

Ben says that as a boy he did a lot of visiting in
other folks' backyards and kitchens. Both his parents
worked; he was the oldest of six brothers and sisters
and spent most of his time as an adolescent setting a
series of good examples for these younger siblings to
follow. He learned to drink coffee in the kitchen at
an early age and came to know what the women at
their kitchen tables were going to say next, and to
say it before they did. Back-porch chatter was a major
ingredient in his education, and he passed on the
information of one age to the next; he became
aggressively gregarious at an early age. He called the
mothers by their first names before he was ten; he
went through a period of shyness at the age of
twelve, but this passed with grammar school. After
that, he says, he was always one of the boys. His father had little time to teach the children how to play
basketball or box, so Ben taught them instead. His
father taught them all to play poker, which he said
was necessary for their survival in the world. His
mother tried as best she could to teach them to sing,
in trios and quartets, but never got much further
than a few church hymns.

Ben's factory is involved in food packaging as well
as drug packaging, and although everything is kept

very clean, it all looks shabbier at night. The hydraulic lift trucks stand at the end of the runway, stuck against the wall like a herd of dirty metal giraffes, gritted jaws aclench. When Ben comes back to where Margaret is sitting, she asks him how big his apartment is. Then she realizes she is being pushy and explains that her children really need a big apartment, and all she can think about lately are apartments and houses. She wants to move to Waukesha because she's got a couple of girl friends there. Ben says he lives with a friend, and it's big enough for them both to move around in.

Margaret tells him she has a friend named Sue who just quit working nights because she said she'd never find another husband working that way. Margaret laughs and says she for one is not worried about getting married again. Another man from the shampoo line comes over, and the conversation between Ben and Margaret ends.

Margaret's a sweet girl, says Ben. He says she knows the score. When Ben was growing up, one thing he learned from the men and women in their kitchens was that it was impossible to run away from the facts of life. Ben says he has always tried to confront things head-on, and not to be hypocritical about his life. He says he has a positive outlook; his is most certainly an affable personality. In his way he is fighting the odds with his life-style. But the stimulation of being an underdog is the sort of stimulation he likes best, and he says that realizing he was homosexual is the best thing that ever happened to him. He says meeting Patrick is the second best.

Patrick mixes in more turpentine to a small mound of cobalt blue on his palette in his studio. He picks up the outlines of the irises of a child's eyes on the left side of the large dark canvas. Immediately he sees that the background behind the figure needs darkening. He unscrews the cap from a tube of chrome yellow, then dabs in the color on the palette next to the blue. He brings the brush to the canvas and continues.

Patrick says he and Ben are both solid citizens. They each work in the night, in their own fashion. Ben says he is not an original the way Patrick is. His own creativity is limited to writing a bit of rhyming verse from time to time. He says that, had things in his own upbringing been different, he still doubts that he would have become any kind of creative artist himself. He is doubly proud of Patrick's work.

Patrick has the face of an angel approaching middle age. As a child, his wide eyes and blond curly hair made him resemble one of those *putti* who are to be seen flying across the church domes of Florence and Siena. His looks were made much of as a child; his mother always tried to show him off to his best advantage, and the result was that his young schoolmates soon found ugly words to define his prettiness. When he grew to be a young man, his looks hardened somewhat. Now, at thirty-eight, his frame is more substantial. He is five feet nine, and his dark blond hair curls in thick ringlets. His lower lip is still petulant as a boy's, but at thirty-eight petulance reads truculence. He begrudges a smile.

A painter's profile evolves over the years. The

forehead keeps bunching at the line of the eyebrows, and the lips keep thrusting upward in a perpetually appraising pout or grimace. The features gather as emotional focus has gathered, all in a clump at mid-face. Patrick painting is stern and vigorous, and so impatient that he yells at the turpentine bottle.

A copy of Gide's *Corydon* lies open beside Patrick's bed. The page he is reading has to do with the individualization of the male animal, citing the fact that the female nightingale is mute, whereas the male sings. Patrick collects such detail. Beneath the hardcover book is an issue of *Science* magazine in which is contained a paper on the songs and chants of the male and female gibbons. A lion stares down at him from his studio wall, one of his few drawings he has ever liked well enough to keep. His painted animals now are more fanciful than lions. He envisions swallows with the lungs of whales.

In his studio there is an hour or so when the moon hangs a few inches above the apartment house next door, a few inches below the window frame on the east wall. The moon climbs as the sun climbs, and Patrick says it gives him a feeling of energy to have it hanging there, in that dark blue rectangle of sky, as his painting night begins. Tonight, Patrick has awakened alone, because Ben has left early to take his nephew his birthday present, and to visit his sister. From the studio he walks to the kitchen and reaches for the coffee pot on its electric pad on the counter. Waking up each afternoon, pulling himself into consciousness, Patrick says he feels as if he's unsticking

himself from flypaper. It takes a half-hour of swill-
ing coffee to get him awake. By the time he walks
into the studio, it is late afternoon. He paints in oils
and there is a bluish tinge to his palette. He thinks
the idea of painting in bright sunlight is extreme. He
likes a nice natural artificial light.

Ben says that for a city so thoroughly Germanic,
Milwaukee is a remarkable combination of conserva-
tism and liberality. He points out that in Milwaukee
the mayor sings. Gemütlichkeit entrances even the
muses.

Patrick never thought he'd find himself living in
Milwaukee. He came to the city ten years before to
attend Layton Art School. As an artist in a competitive environment, Patrick says he is a failure every
day he doesn't receive some tangible acknowledgment of his success. He says it mockingly, but not
without a tone of conviction. A buyer in an art gal-
lery, or in his studio, asks how long it took to do a
certain painting, and he tells him thirty-eight years.
He is aware that his paintings are judged first by
their general commercial success, and then by his
own highly personal standards. His paintings are
rather too harsh to enjoy a popular reputation in a
city that prefers the familiar in its artwork. But he is
respected as an artist, and he has a scrapbook of
paragraphs that attest to his worth and reputation.
And he has a partner who buoys him up and says
that he's the best artist around.

For every painter it is different: when you sell a
painting, you sell your life. You sell your sense of
order. The cash is reinforcement; the main idea is

that others value your sense of cohesion, detail, and
design enough to pay for it. But the better it is, the
more personal it is. Making a living from doing the
best you can at what you value most is a luxury and
Patrick knows it.

Patrick has traveled. When he was young, he saw
the blue monkeys of Thera painted on the walls of
an Athens museum; he inspected the elephant in
front of the church of Minerva in Rome. If his circumstances were different, he might be living in the
artists' colony on Corfu, or keeping a house in Crete.
As it is, he lives in Milwaukee.

The apartment is long and brightly lit with floor
lamps; the main hallway, carpeted with an old Ha-
madan runner, opens up to the large studio room
and the bedroom beyond. There is a sink in the studio, and a toilet, but the sink is used mainly for
cleaning out brushes. The living room and dining
room are at the front of the building, with the
kitchen off the front door on the left. Patrick says he
spends an enormous amount of time on the rug,
walking back and forth from the studio to the
kitchen.

Taking a break at midnight, he stands in the
kitchen, watching a movie on Channel 4. Charles
Boyer is interviewing a group of girls for the job of
hat-check girl and cigarette girl in a restaurant he is
about to open in New York. The movie is *History Is
Made at Night*. It is an old movie, and the decor is
high deco. Jean Arthur moves somewhere in the

wings of the plot, breathlessly rearranging her life to match Boyer's.

In the living room off the kitchen there is a large double glass window. In the morning the sun comes down from the northeastern sky and collects in dappled puddles on the polished wood floor. The morning sun is something neither of the men who live in the apartment ever see much of.

When two people live together and one of them is better at nights than days, and his partner has always been the reverse, the metre of the relationship defines itself early on. Living in the night is symbolic for many people; it represents an achievement, rather than an accommodation.

Patrick has always preferred the night, because for him it is the most private time, and he needs privacy. He creates with his back to the crowd. Ben grew up on a daytime schedule, and only since he has been living with Patrick has he come to make the night his territory as well. It is not only his work at the factory, but his time afterward, when the two of them are at home in the apartment together, that he values.

"Try to remember that this table is reserved permanently," says Boyer. "And that these flowers are to be changed daily." He turns to the giggling hatcheck girls, frowning slightly, arching one eyebrow. "None of this," he continues, rolling his eyes and clucking his tongue, parodying their flirting manner. "Don't forget. You are here to check hats and nothing else." The pillbox hats bob, and the girls run off screen. There is a commercial. Patrick flips the dial to a Chicago channel and listens to the last of a news broadcast. He splits an English muffin and sticks it into the toaster oven. In a few minutes he removes it and covers the two surfaces with whipped cream cheese, then sits down at the butcher-block kitchen table to eat.

A night apartment is difficult in any town. In a town like Milwaukee, which prizes daylight and industry, it is especially difficult to ignore the day. But their friends don't call Ben and Patrick before noon, and the sound that comes in from the street is minimal in their suburban neighborhood. The two men feel they have their lives worked out relatively well, and that they are in control, most of the time, of their surroundings. The studio and the apartment around it come into their own at night. The shape of a room changes when there is no sunlight to diffuse the impact of certain objects. The axis shifts with the change of light source; areas that would be lit and given prominence during the daylight are at night only negative spaces in the background. A shoe, a straw hamper, a long white vase filled with irises: all these look different under electricity. The foreground and background keep changing at night.

From the air over Milwaukee, a pilot of a four-seater looks down at the city as he prepares to land at Timmerman Airport. He is logging night hours for his instrument rating. Night flying exhilarates him, and once he has landed he will drive from

the airport to his advertising design studio downtown, there to work till dawn on an idea that has occurred to him at seventeen hundred feet.

Ben drives home from the factory at 12:30 A.M.
He drives out along the Lake and follows it north
past the Art Center, along the park. It takes him a
few blocks farther north than is necessary, and he
turns south again at Oakland, arriving home with a
slight crunch in the gravel driveway. He brings in a
six-pack of Heinemann's and a kilo of yoghurt that
he has bought at the all-night Open Pantry, and
Margaret's spider plant.
  Patrick, painting in the studio, doesn't hear him
come in. He scowls at the canvas, at the human and
animal figures before him, rubbing out the form of a
bat from the background.

A woman named Carolyn sits in her bedroom a
few blocks away on the north side of town, learning
her lines for a Little Theatre production of *Comedy
of Errors.* Her husband, who works during the day at
the university audiovisual department, catches his
breath in his sleep and turns muttering to the wall.
She whispers to herself the words of her lines,
widening her eyes with each speech.

Patrick believes in Art. He believes in his own talent, but it isn't mere ego that keeps him in his studio
with no fellow workers to shore up his confidence
when it lags. He is his own student and his own
teacher, and believes he is doing best what he alone
does best. He says he has to paint in his own terms

and at his own pace. He likes the idea of producing art in a world of industry, going against the tide of computerized statements of order, of xerox duplications and pocket calculators and media newspeak. He likes to paint with a low murmuring sound as the background in his studio, a radio voice turned down so low the words are indistinguishable.

Patrick says two is the most obvious number of the night. One is the number of the sun, alone and indomitable; whereas two is the number of cooperation, of working things out. Patrick and Ben feel closest at night, most in harmony. Patrick's mother doesn't see things as her son does; she really wishes he didn't love Ben. Her idea of harmony between people doesn't include quite so much between members of the same sex. She thinks that homosexual love profanes her own; Patrick says that her attitude causes him grief, but that he has over the years learned not to expect anything else from her. He is an only child, born in Pennsylvania, and his father has been dead for some time. His mother lives in a condominium in Boca Raton, Florida, and writes him letters.

Patrick doesn't say homosexuality's better, but he doesn't say it's worse. Patrick's mother writes that in Boca Raton the sun never sets; she wishes he would come down and stay with her. So many pretty girls on the beach. Lots of galleries to show in. Patrick's mother never lets up. He says, they never let you get through to them that you love another man. He admits, though, that most of the time things really aren't so bad, except that a man can save the life of an American president and still be shunned by his own family when he is reported to be homosexual. Patrick says it's a long way from the millennium, as far as public attitudes toward homosexuality go.

Ben describes himself as being a simple boy with simple pleasures. He likes beer, but he would rather drink white wine. Patrick smokes, and doesn't drink much at all. Patrick once read an article that said the process of dreaming was depressed by the ingestion of alcohol; he thinks alcohol may interfere with the visual network of the memory, and he avoids it for that reason. Ben reminds him that the jury is still out concerning the effect of marijuana on dreaming, but Patrick doesn't suppose the one drug is nearly so harsh as the other.

The two men go out to the bars of the city infrequently, mainly on the weekend. They are perceived as a couple, perhaps less often perceived as a pair. They have been together seven years and intend to go on forever.

Ben has worked in the real world all his life. He takes a vicarious pleasure in Patrick's work in the imagination. When he first came to Milwaukee, Patrick worked in the window display department of the Boston Store downtown. He didn't mind the work; there was some challenge in the arrangement of gloves and bicycles, the placement of cocktail glasses and styrofoam snow. But his painting at night wasn't wonderful in that period. He believes he works best when painting is his sole occupation. He quit the job when he realized that only his older paintings were selling, and none of his new.

Ben and Patrick's union rests on a string. They have never stood in a church and said, Till death us do part. They never would. Nothing legal or familial holds them together; they have simply chosen to spend their lives together. The string slackens or grows taut, and they do what they can to keep their balance.

Two people together can hold fast to an ideal more easily than one person alone. The painter creates only out of his own psyche, only through his own physical and emotional tools, from his own rarefied spirit. But his lover enhances his spirit, and by reinforcing his life reinforces his art. Wives of writers, husbands of poets, the lovers of each; these make up the armor that shields the artist and enables him or her to produce.

We're a set, says Patrick. He thinks using the term roommates after the age of twenty-five is somewhat puerile. Mates, by itself, has a solid ring. Lover is a temporary term; he says he doesn't use it much anymore. We are just good friends, he says, facetiously. Lover is a word written in lipstick on a gilt-flecked mirror. Lover is what you have when you have something else as well—for those who don't, whose lives turn on each other as on a common spindle, lover as a word is strangely hollow.

Patrick has ambitions, but his ambitions are grounded in reality. He knows more than Ben

knows that if they lived in Chicago or Los Angeles or
New York their lives would be very different. His
profession is secure in Milwaukee and the reputation
he enjoys—though it circulates among a smaller circle of opinion than he might like—is a source of
stimulation for him. The two men have worked out
their lives by chipping away places in the rock of
Milwaukee, until they have found acceptable quarters.

The idea of changing one's life completely every
seven years or so is attractive, but neither of them
gets very far in his own speculative fantasy.

Ben's is the more conservative nature. He values
order and, of the two, is the more resistant to
change. But he also responds to style; there is a chair
in the bedroom they paid $500 for, which is a lot to
pay on North Downer Avenue in Milwaukee, for a
chair.

Patrick feels that each night he passes brings him
closer to some sort of final aesthetic reality. Each
four-by-eight or six-by-six stretch of canvas is necessary to the next; it is the process of his art that matters to him. He says that the verb *painting* is more
important than the noun; the production of objects
to be used by the eye is too finite a process for him,
in and of itself. Patrick says that when he is painting
well, it is like courting his own past.

Ben says that Patrick grew up expecting everything, and that he grew up expecting nothing. He
says it philosophically, in the kitchen at 2:00 A.M.,
with a smile that Patrick returns from where he

stands next to the refrigerator. It is a glib statement
of psychologies to which neither objects.

Ben has put the six-pack in the refrigerator, and
now arranges the plant on the window sill in the living room. Patrick goes back to the studio and adds
some oil to his palette. He hums along with Mama
Cass as he works. He has turned the volume up,
which is unusual for him, and jabs at the canvas as
he sings.

The canvas is resolved in a long thin swipe of blue
along the arm of the principal figure. Patrick pulls
back the brush from the figure's elbow. He scruti-
nizes the painting and steps back a few paces from it.
Admitting that a painting is finished is the most difficult and at the same time the most exhilarating
moment. The balance has to be just right. He has
been working on this canvas for three weeks, and he
is happy with it.

Ben comes in with a bottle of beer and stands with
his arm around Patrick's shoulder, the two of them
looking at the stretch of bright canvas.

Across town, Margaret's mother watches as Jean
Arthur steps up onto a gangplank. In her small living room the old woman nurses a glass of cream
sherry. The fingers of her left hand find the back of
her cat, and she scratches the old animal slowly, patiently. She watches the actress move across the television screen, dissolving into a blur of grey.

Patrick cleans his brushes, moving the wet black
bristles back and forth as if they are the tails of fish.

He has been given the advantage of competing only against himself, in his own terms, and at a moment of satisfaction such as this, he says he feels quite fortunate. He is not really an intellectual; he doesn't objectify himself, nor remove himself theoretically from his work. He is his work. He wrings out the ends of the dark brushes, working the wet hairs free of each other. Then he places them on a paper towel beside the sink. Ben comes back in and hands him a joint of marijuana. You deserve it, he says, smiling. The two men sit on the floor for some time in front of the canvas, smoking and talking.

In the living room, an hour later, the first faint light of day comes through the plant-hung window. Heat comes on through the steam pipes, sputtering and gargling through the speckled network of rust and iron that is the building's plumbing. Outside, the traffic begins to honk itself awake. In the packaging plant the machines are silent; the day plant manager, coming in early, discovers the security guard dozing in his chair, a golf magazine spread open in his lap.

The sunlight shines in through the window of the apartment, gradually moving down the shelves of plants. It reaches the small spider plant and colors the sharp pointed leaves greenish yellow. Finally, in golden density, sunlight fills the empty room.

AKA Gloria

New Yorkers gather at night in neon-lit pools, like exotic deepwater fish. New York at night is a city of sensation and stimulation, with people rubbing against each other, in bars and public rooms, and theatres and restaurants, until they glow.

Gloria lives in Manhattan. She is almost always up by noon and home again by the following dawn. Gloria has a flared nostril and a smile like Ava Gardner's. She works as an actress and as a dancer, and there are nights when she works at both jobs, rushing from one to the other. When Gloria wakes up, the sun has long since passed its forty-minute appearance in her tiny garden, and the grey sky matches the grey brick buildings on either side of her apartment. In her small bathroom she looks long in the mirror over the sink. The appearance of her face in profile is very different from its appearance full-face. In profile she is stark; from dead ahead in close-up, she is warm and inviting.

She decides on the look she prefers to feature before she does her makeup, before she combs out her dark hair. Starkness is professional: a Bergman grimace, the face on a Greek coin, the profile of the California coastline north of Marin County. She turns full-face. Warmth is for getting into and out of tight squeezes. Warmth is for comfort and ease, for the time at the end of the brightly lit tunnel that is her night.

She spends the first half-hour she's awake brewing and drinking a pot of Frauen tea, nibbling at a batch of tofu—Chinese bean curd—which she has made two days before, and assuring her dog, Alice, that it's going to be a wonderful day. She feels some residual guilt, left over from her up-with-the-larks California girlhood, about sleeping through the entire morning, but that relaxes after the merest second of panic.

She checks in with her agency, and with her answering service; then she calls New Jersey to find out about her booking for the week following. It is a struggle, and a wrench of ego, to each day every day throw herself out to the sea of casting directors, agents, producers, and club owners. But it is an effort of will and gumption that Gloria has in her years of New York living learned to make. She does it now with a minimum of fuss, because thinking about it too much would be counterproductive. After an hour of telephoning, she swallows two tablespoons of protein powder, does twenty sit-ups, and looks at her life.

As an actress, she has worked twice in the last three years in a Broadway show. Her first appear-

ance was as Asuri, the sinuous native dancer in *The
Desert Song* at the Uris; the second was as Mazeppa,
the stripper with the bugle in Angela Lansbury's
Gypsy. Earl Wilson headlined his column the day
after *The Desert Song* opened by proclaiming her,
among other things, the Stomach of the Year. He
gave her four paragraphs. Both the *News* and the
Post reported that she stopped the show, and in fact
she did. As a whirling, glittering phenomenon of the
desert, she performed a belly dance that brought the
audience to its feet. The week of the opening, she
was drawn in caricature by Hirschfeld in the *New
York Times* theatre section. She has had a Nina con-
cealed in her skirt. She is getting there.

But her career is not at the moment up to the level
of either of these stellar performances. It is now two
years after the *Gypsy* Broadway production, and she
is in the process of deciding whether or not to take
the role again in Florida. Her agent is asking for five
hundred a week; she imagines she'll probably get a
bit less, but as there's a free hotel room thrown in,
it's an agreeable enough proposition. She thinks
she'll most probably do the show, even though it
means being out of the city over the holidays. The
tour includes Christmas Eve in Miami Beach, a pros-
pect she views with little enthusiasm.

She is usually out of the apartment by three thirty
or four o'clock in the afternoon, moving into the
night at an accelerating walk. She finds she has to
pace herself when she is working both as Gloria
Rossi, actress, and as Zitana, belly-dancer extraordi-
naire. The night is where the theatrical action is; no-

body envisions her name in lights against the back-drop of a daytime sky. She seldom gets to bed before three, no matter what she is doing. She thinks the meat of the night is the hour before midnight and the two hours after. She likes being at Sardi's or Joe Allen's during the half-hour the Broadway shows let out, seeing the audience and the performers relaxing and celebrating at the same time. She says she is addicted to show business.

For the last week and a half, she has been dying every other night at 9:42 P.M., a scream offstage at the American Place Theatre on 46th Street. There, she is slaughtered by a group of vengeful Puritans for being an Indian whore. That is her billing in the program: Indian Whore. In the second play of the evening she is The Prostitute and wears a see-through plastic skirt and an enormous white wig of the period—the mid-eighteenth century in the American colonies. Along with her spoken lines, she is required as well to sing a song about law and lust and perversity.

She must be at the theatre a half-hour before curtain each night the plays are on. The first goes on at eight, the second at ten, and as the two of them make up one repertory bill, and a third play another, she needn't be at the theatre every night and can take belly-dancing jobs elsewhere. Her dancing takes her out of town in shorter spurts than do her acting roles. She does a weekend in New Jersey or the Poconos, but more often she works in clubs in Manhattan or on Long Island, one night at a time. She also dances on cruise ships, traveling first class

for ten days in the islands of the Caribbean. Generally, her careers move at tangents to one another;
the coincidence of *Desert Song* was a one-of-a-kind
meshing of the two.

Onstage and off, Gloria keeps a clean house. She
isn't what one would call rigid about the subject, but
she does like things neat. She is clean and she is
thorough. She is much more apt to overwater than
underwater her plants. Her acting is thorough, too.

As a prostitute, she is not totally believable onstage. Perhaps this is because she comes across clean.
She isn't quite dirty enough. She is what her acting
teacher calls a mischief. She is at her most successful
in portrayals of unique types, characters for whom
there are no prototypes. She is what the world calls a
perfectionist, both in her work and in her life, and
she is constantly improving herself. Yet with each
improvement, there is a further specialization that
moves her away from type, from readily identifiable
cliché. The dark ingenue who is a mischief, who
learns every craft she attempts, is not someone who
can sing "My Heart Belongs to Daddy" and get away
with it. Her wiles show. (Currently, she is doing a
series of eighteen-second snatches of songs for her
acting class, snatches from identifiable numbers,
amusing but not too cute. Her singing coach has ad-
vised her that it is a mistake to do a Connie Stevens
number, "I'm the Girl Friend of the Whirling Der-
vish." He also says to forget "Gimmick," the Mazeppa song from *Gypsy*. What there is about her that
is fresh and witty is what he wants to emphasize. She
is between genres, really: a Dark Lady who is also an

ingenue. Her acting coach says she could be an
American Kay Kendall.)

Gloria is always willing to change her image.

She likes the name Antonia—her father's name was
Anthony—and is thinking of changing over after
these thirty years as Gloria. She thinks maybe it will
change her luck. She gets furious with herself for
what she calls the Will to Fail, the perverse drive in
her that makes her twenty minutes late for a Bertolucci
audition and keeps her talking on the phone to her
friend Susannah during the hour her agent is sup-
posed to be calling her about a *Trojan Woman* tryout
she did the week before. It comes and it goes, this
perversity; sometimes it is followed by a week of fast-
ing, or a month of sexual abstinence. Other times it
evaporates in the space of a taxi ride uptown, or a
night on the town with a diamond merchant from
Kuwait. It is when she is working, and working well,
that she is at her best. A few nights before, she did a
benefit in New Jersey for a Lebanese group, working
for half her regular fee since it was a charitable en-
deavor. They threw exactly $455 at her feet, which,
instead of going into her own sequined pocket, went
directly to the relief fund. Ah well, she sighs, charity
is charity. They might, however, have given her an
extra ten dollars. After the benefit she rode back
into Manhattan with the Arab musicians in their van,
stopping for coffee and more music at the Tiffany
Diner off the New Jersey Turnpike. Coming across
the George Washington Bridge at 5:00 A.M., the
skyline of Manhattan looked to her like a series of
enormous sandstone caves, like the cliffs of Mesa

Verde she remembers visiting as a child. There is
something about the light refracted through the mist
over the Hudson, the lights of the office buildings
and hotels flickering through it, that gives the island
an ancient tribal look. Gloria feels secure in Manhattan. She says that at this point in her life, she can't
really think about living anywhere else. Gloria the
actress blooms in Manhattan like a night-blooming
cereus in a lunarium; her performing psyche thrives
in the environment of the city, drawing stimulation
from it at every breath. She says she'd be happiest if
she didn't have to sleep at all, but her athlete's body
needs its periods of restoration, and relaxation, her
mind its hours of subconscious drifting.

Two afternoons a week she goes to a therapist on
Central Park West who encourages her to relive certain moments of tension in her early life, and to
open up and release them by acting out, screaming
out, her remembered feelings. She is hoarse and exhausted after these sessions, but she considers both
her time and her psyche well spent.

There are contradictions in her two careers. Gloria
the actress is truth and strength and good timing.
Gloria the dancer is a bundle of lies: soft lies, fluttering untruths, hard-edged rhinestone and paste de-
ceptions designed to enchant the eye and excite the
groin. Gloria dancing is all in-moving gesture; her
body under light is a bubbling focus of centripetal
force. She deceives by miming vulnerability.

Neither actress nor dancer is visible at mid-after-
noon, however. Until she brings herself into focus,
Gloria the schlepper is the Gloria that prevails. She

moves about her apartment tentatively, slowly
shedding the clumsiness of sleep, talking to Alice,
her enormous black poodle. Gradually, she assem-
bles an outfit for the evening, for the theatre and for
she knows not what after. She dresses carefully, as
befits a rising star: a tailored black jacket and slacks,
a silver chain, shoes from Charles Jourdan, a Ralph
Lauren scarf. Her hair is black and curled almost as
tightly as Alice's. She has another long look in the
mirror, attentive to every detail of her appearance.
Today, her eyes are good, and no line betrays her
brow. She brushes on a touch of kohl, while stretching her upper palate to the tune of "Un Bel Di."
Alice cocks her head at the sound.

You really are only as big as your last hit. Gloria
has touched a certain pinnacle in her career, and it is
difficult not to want to dance on that pinnacle forever. She is impatient with her career and wants to
get on with it. She tries to do everything she can to
get on with it. Gloria is already playing herself in the
story of her life. The thing about New York City is
that you can never stay completely on top of it all the
time. If you get on top of it once, or twice, you're
ahead of the millions and millions who clamber up
from below you. The only way for them to get up is
if you get down, and nobody ever wants to get down.
You keep yourself as fit as you can; you keep everything ready to step back into the spotlight.
    Her moon is in Leo, and all the other planets in
her chart are in fire signs as well. Her ascendant is
Libra, her sun sign is Scorpio. It is a sign of perse-
verance and impulse. She finds that she is often at-

tracted to Libra men. A director who pulls out of her
more than she thinks she can give, and who stresses
discipline above all, is best, as far as she is concerned.

Her refrigerator is a hymn to Adelle Davis. There
is a compartmentalized tray that covers half a shelf
with pellets and tablets and pills. Power B Complex
is a dusky translucent orange. Vitamin C is ivory,
yeast is tan. There are red and orange and yellow
tablets piled against each other like candy corn or M
and M's, and granular whites and sticky whites and
capsules in three different shades of pink.

She has lately learned how to make tofu and keeps
a bowl of it on the second shelf. She makes it from
bean powder and hangs it in a mesh sling until it
forms a ball of just the right texture. Since she took
up belly-dancing in the years before *Desert Song*, her
diet has been a mixture of babaganoosh and wheat
germ, a blend of the exotic and the spartan. She
knows how to cook quail and olives, just as she
knows how to make her own tofu. She is five foot
eight, and her best weight is a pound or two under
140.

Alice eats what Gloria eats, except the protein
powder is the less expensive variety: a bowl of protein flakes with some soy oil sprinkled over it, and a
teaspoon of powder mixed in. Gloria has been a veg-
etarian for four years, so there are no meat scraps
from the table.

Alice is enormous and black, a full-size poodle
which Gloria and her ex-husband acquired a year
after they were married, while they were living
on Bank Street in Greenwich Village. The three of

them bore a litter of twelve together, an experience
Gloria is not ready to face again. Alice is of excellent
stock, and the puppies were not difficult to sell, but
there was a month of weaning in the dining room,
and the smell of puppy urine became tiresome. Alice
was a good mother, Gloria says, but she is now, like
her owner, on the pill. Gloria will one day also be a
good mother, Gloria hopes. The pill is for now.

Once every two weeks Gloria takes the IRT out to
Brooklyn to see her iridologist, who makes sure her
system is generally as it should be. He has put her on
a diet containing no fats or oils; she has also given
up sugar, and her body, for all its occasional quirks
and muscular miseries, is still a remarkably efficient
machine most of the time. An iridologist is able to
see what's wrong with a person's physical harmony
by inspecting the iris of the eye. Gloria's iris is pres-
ently a circle of good health.

Her back, however, is a little out of synchro-
nization and she plans a trip up to her gymnasium
on 57th Street for a few light lifts and some heavy
steam before going on to the theatre at seven.

But as she's going out the door, the phone rings
and after a moment's hesitation—should she or
should she not let her recorded voice reply to
it?—she picks it up. A photographer friend on 39th
Street needs her to model her hands for a drug ad
he's shooting; the regular model has canceled—will
she help him out?

Serendipity, serendipity—of course she'll help him
out; naturally she's getting the same pay the model

would, right? Right. She decides to forget the gym,
hangs up the phone, locks the iron terrace doors
($125 apiece to put in, after she learned from neigh-
bors that the apartment had been burglarized repeatedly the year before. Ah, the Greek landlord has
said, raising his eyebrows and his palms to heaven,
Life in the city, my child, is never easy. Finally, he
has agreed to pay for one door if she will pay for the
other, and he happens to have a cousin who will be
happy to install them, cheap. This agreement,
reached six months before, has a week ago resulted
in the doors' installation, by a cousin of a cousin,
unsmiling, wondering where his tip is. The doors are
black wrought iron, with space enough between the
decorative whirls for a dozen nimble youths to slip
through), says her good-byes to Alice, and is gone.

The advertising panels on bus stop shelters in New
York City light up at 5:00 P.M. Riding uptown, she
passes one at 28th Street, the light switching on with
a snap.

On 39th Street the photographer and the art
director are deep in discussion over whether to shoot
the hand holding the pills from a horizontal or a vertical angle. Gloria relaxes on a batik chair, off to the
left of the shooting area, her beringed hands slowly
turning a copy of *Uomo Vogue*.

She reads Italian, not because she learned it at
home as a child—she didn't—but because she lived
in Rome as a struggling film actress for two years
and had to pick it up in order to get by. She learned
a lot about getting past the men on New York's 14th
Street by pursuing her way down Rome's Via della
Scrofa, and she says casting directors in Manhattan

are pale imitations of the suave and lecherous denizens of Cinecittà. She has photographs from her
Roman period in the late sixties, smiling, pouting,
holding up a stuffed teddy bear, arms raised and
framing her hair, cheap and seductive. The photos
are an embarrassment to her, but they remind her of
the period, and all that was good about it—she
hadn't yet married, and she and her friend Susannah lived together in what they thought was a rea-
sonably respectable pensione. There were other ex-
patriate friends. It was a good time. Neither spoke
much of the language yet; there were cheery and in-
articulate hellos to the other women, all of them Italian, when they passed in the pensione halls.

One night, an English gentleman in his fifties
knocked on her door and asked, in Ruth Draper
Italian, what she would do for 5,000 lire. She
screamed, he left—amid profuse apologies—and
when Susannah came home, the two young women
carted their belongings out of the pensione amid the
derisive laughter of the prostitutes who, it turned
out, had been living there and working there all
along. Gloria says she knows from whores. Her onstage portrayals of them are often stitched in malice.
But she knows women who are in the life whom
she likes a great deal, so she is not a prude. Not exactly. She believes in services rendered.

There is a word in Italian, which she has heard
used in Rome to describe certain older women. The
word is *tardona,* and it means someone who, later in
life than is seemly, consorts with men younger than
herself. Gloria is decades away from such a label, but
sees it rising up out of the mists of her future like a
warning iceberg. Younger men are, well, younger.

They are more insistent, less considerate; they say
they are blinded by their passion, and in some mem-
orable cases, perhaps, they are. Gloria says there is
something to be said for a thunderingly linear pro-
gression, and something to be said for a circular
route. The artistic psyche thrives on variety; Gloria
sees many men, and some of them are older than
she, and some of them are younger. Age becomes irrelevant early on in the theatre.

Gloria thinks that she had a rather too rigorously
religious upbringing. She grew up believing that
God heard every word. In the fifth grade she was expelled for two weeks by the sisters of her school.
There was a major earthquake in the San Francisco
Bay area that year, and she and her classmates were
instructed to stay where they were and to say their
rosaries when it began to shake the school. Amid the
rumbling, the wall of the schoolroom was crossed by
a jagged crack, like an enormous black finger writing
across it. Gloria, when she saw the crack, yelled
something extremely disrespectful about the church
at large and urged everybody out of the schoolroom,
into the open. The room was not destroyed; therefore Gloria was adjudged to be clearly in the wrong
and was expelled.

One of the sisters had earlier that year sent her
home from the Hallowe'en parade, because the skirt
of her costume was too short. It was an orange and
black cheerleader's outfit, with small pom-poms and
a black tu-tu skirt. Her mother had been working on
it for weeks, but that fact mattered little. The costume and she in it were prohibited from marching.

She once built a grotto of mirror and rock, quite

the best grotto in the parish, and was given as a prize a statue of the Virgin to fill it. She remembers being in an ecstasy whenever it was time to go on retreat.

She has now transferred the disciplines of the church to the discipline of the body, reads as much as she can on Science of the Mind, and knows a good many Edgar Cayce remedies by heart. She has had her hands read by experts and her feet as well. Five years ago a woman reading her character from the soles of her feet told her alarming things about her future. Gloria is open to all positive influences, no matter where or how they occur. She tries to get up to the Cathedral of Saint John the Divine at 110th Street for the sessions with Sufi chanting; her dancing self responds to the hypnotic chanting and the contained abandon. Sometimes, Gloria thinks her belly-dancing has kept her sane. The gods dance in a polyglot pantheon for her. The golden Saints of Santa Maria in Rome's Trastevere; Siva rampant on an Indian medallion; temple dancers, fetish dancers; exultant whirling dervishes—they all have something to whisper in her ear, and she is always ready to listen.

Gloria's numerologist has told her that whereas the name she now uses adds up to a six, a lovely blue number with lots in its favor, should she change Gloria to Antonia she would then be a four, a number with slightly more problematical aspects. Four is the number of eccentricity, and of unorthodox rebellion, whereas six is extremely magnetic in character, tending toward the romantic. Her acting career up till now has been conducted as a six (as Zit-

ana, she adds up to a one, which is overwhelmingly
positive and forceful), and to step across into the
land of the fours would be, numerologically speaking,
a serious move. It would mean moving away from
Venus, and assuming the attributes of Uranus, he in-
forms her. Should she do it? It is a problem. She
tried Antonia out on one casting director who said it
sounded as if she were an authoress, an image she
does not particularly wish to convey. Further compli-
cating the switch is her sun sign, Scorpio, and the
fact that she was born in the Year of the Dog. Her
birth number totals two, with the day itself adding
up to a seven, which is what her last name alone also
totals. Her married name, first and last combined,
was an eight, an infelicitous number compared to
her working number, six. Her numerologist thinks
perhaps she ought to leave well enough alone.

Friends take Gloria under their wing. She inspires
trust and confidence, but she also inspires compas-
sion because what she is attempting to do with her
life is so difficult. To keep battling obscurity night
after night, onstage and off, is a feat to be admired.
Her mother helps her along with a fur coat at
Christmas, an offer to help her with her rent. Her
father is no longer living, but she has two brothers
still in California, pursuing their own lives. She has
cousins in Las Vegas, and uncles in Genoa, and one
of her aunts is the mother superior in a convent outside Genoa. Before she left Rome, and the lukewarm
puddle that her career there was becoming, she
stayed at the convent for ten days. She returned to
the United States and to California, and then she

married her husband and the two of them settled in
Greenwich Village, each of them taking classes and
working as best they could. They split up after six
years.

Gloria moved out of the house on Bank Street and
took Alice with her. She and her former husband see
each other, but not frequently. Gloria is not often
blinded by love. She is blinded by talent, and making
love with someone whose talent dazzles you often
passes for love. In the night it is not only one's self
that is enhanced by a dark background. Gloria has
felt her heart chewing on itself while watching more
than one great talent from the wings. Actors under
light are a focus of energy and enthusiasm that is seldom unattractive, and Gloria has had an affair or
two with an onstage companion. But Gloria has been
onstage most of her life, so she's entitled.

Gloria's friends in New York are always suggesting
dramatic or comedic numbers for her to do. She
takes their suggestions as often as she can; a few
more details in her repertoire couldn't hurt.

She would love to act the title role of Colette's vag-
abond, Renée. She learns more about acting as she
learns more about living; more and more details ac-
crue to her, the older and wiser she gets. Gypsy wis-
dom comes to her in fits and snatches; she has gotten
to know a lot about jewelry, for instance, since she's
been dancing for Arabs. She has begun to bite
pearls.

Everyone knows how tough it is for an actress in
New York: girls who studied Stanislavski do ads for
stannous flouride and are happy to get the work. As

an actress, you say yes to everything, automatically, because the chances are the job will somehow fall through anyway, somewhere along the line. You don't even let yourself *think* a part is possible until you've been to a second or third call-back audition. And then you're still at the mercy of whatever the producer had for lunch. You know you're all wrong for the part your agent sends you up for, but still you go, and hand them your photos, and tell them what you've done, and swirl out the door of the office as if it couldn't matter less whether you get the part or not.

People know who Gloria is after *Gypsy* and *Desert Song*, but she is younger and softer than the roles in these shows imply, so when she's not tough enough to play a wrestler or old enough to play a weathered hooker, they feign surprise. But you're so much prettier than we expected, dear. You're really much too young.

Gloria is pushing thirty and doesn't feel she's too young, for anything. But she'd like to get back to playing serious roles and is learning Nina in *The Seagull* for her acting class. She has the speeches on flash-cards, which she takes with her to the gym, to learn in the sauna, in a taxi, anyplace an idle moment occurs.

The photographer and the art director decide on a horizontal rather than a vertical approach to her hands, finally, and she moves in under the lights and the black reflector umbrellas, draping her wrists across the muslin-covered sawhorse that serves as a prop. It has started to rain, and the sound on the studio's overhead skylight is dull and hypnotic. The skylight is a stained-glass plaque with two female figures flanking a central medallion. In the medallion there is a rising sun behind four small boats; over the scene on a dirty golden banner is the word *Excelsior*. The art director wants to know how Gloria got started in acting. It's a question she is seldom asked, and she pauses before answering, her body immobile under the lights.

"I don't know, actually. I suppose dressing up in my mother's clothes when I was about eight. . . . I don't remember ever saying to myself, 'You're going to be an actress.' It just happened."

The director is smiling at her, professionally, competently. The photographer twists the vial of pills in her right hand; the print is reflecting too much light. The shot is for a drug company, the pills are for asthma attacks.

"Once you've been on Broadway, though, it becomes a little easier, you know. Now they know what I've done; I don't have to start from scratch every time at an audition. . . ."

The lights flash, and the photographer takes a Polaroid snapshot to make sure there's not too much bounce.

Broadway. The art director's attention is now focused. Maybe he's seen her in something? She tells him the roles she's done and he grins with pleasure. At the Winter Garden, right? He saw it with his wife and five children, loved it, really loved it. Isn't that amazing? He blows his nose. He looks at her with renewed interest, at an Actress, not merely an actress. He tells her that his fifteen-year-old daughter wants to go on the stage.

Gloria gives him the only advice there is to give; she tells him that the best thing to do is to get a good agent. She doesn't add that there is no such thing.

The rain abates after twenty minutes, and the art director says he'd really like to stay and talk to her, but that it's after six and since they've got the shots they need (the photographer has been working as they talk), he's got to run. After the shooting, the photographer apologizes for not being able to pay her then and there. He says he'll send her a check. Gloria has a half-hour before she's due at the theatre, and since it's only a few blocks away from the studio and since it's no longer raining when she gets out on the street, she decides to walk over to Ninth Avenue. She hurries along the wet pavement to the all-night vegetable stalls there, to pick up some herbs which she can stick in her bag: some thyme, some dill, and a clump of basil if they still have any. She walks the two blocks, past the Port Authority Bus Terminal, and finds dill at the first neon-lit stall, basil but no thyme at the second. She likes the old Italian men who run the stalls; and she likes still knowing enough Italian to understand what they say to each other about her as she fishes in her bag for change and waits for them to give her her small packages. She can cope with that kind of appraisal; she's heard it all her life. The fact that they don't know she understands them makes their remarks all the more flattering, if rather overstated. It's all right. They are old enough to be her father, her uncles, even her grandfather. She can't linger to look for thyme, and crosses the street and hurries along 42nd Street, toward the theatre.

Downtown, the telephone rings in her apartment,
and her recorded voice comes on to urge the caller
not to hang up, to leave a name and number. Her
voice is calm, nearly languid. It is difficult to fit the
voice to the strong, focused body striding past the
bookstores and junk merchants of Times Square.
The body is a flaming powerhouse; the voice is all
vulnerability. Both are Gloria, in the same second of
time.

If she has to travel along 42nd Street, from Eighth
Avenue to Seventh, as she does tonight, she tells herself that she is passing a *tableau vivant,* the midway of
a carnival, anything to give it the air of the pictur-
esque, instead of the dangerous and seedy. It is difficult. The street is perhaps the most depressing
street in the world to walk along alone. The assault
of pure sensation is everywhere. Black teen-agers in
tennis shoes and turned-down straw hats step out
from beneath theatre marquees and tell her they'll
show her a really heavy time; white men and brown
men and men with straggling moustaches push their
closed hands at her, murmuring, THC: How about
some dynamite reefer; Try some coke, lady; Boss
mes here; Blotter. She wishes she didn't look like she
might use it, although she doesn't really mind the
offers. But a man in an ancient overcoat leans out of
a pizza stand doorway and hisses, Give me some
head, you jive turkey bitch, and then she *is* upset and
hurries on her way. His voice has an edge of mad-
ness in it, the blur of his body to the left as she
passes him is like an enormous albino bat hanging in
the wooden door frame. It is an image she doesn't
need in her head, doesn't need in her repertoire.

She would like to, and probably could, rip him apart with her gloved hands.

She finds herself sympathetic to men like the old Italians whom she should probably despise as much for their remarks as she does the young junkie for his. It is all in the manner of approach. When a Sun Myung Moon follower thrusts himself on her at the corner of Seventh Avenue and begins his spiel, she makes the sign of the cross in his face and bares her teeth at him, upsetting for the moment even his myopic equanimity. Most of the time, the animal she pretends to be as she walks through the streets convinces the muggers and drunks and the men who press against her on corners that they'd do best to back off and leave her alone. She passes beneath the news banner on the Allied Tower and turns north.

Her strength and agility saved her life in the Village a Christmas ago; at an intersection not far from Sheridan Square, a car came hurtling through a stoplight and struck down a man who, like Gloria, had looked up to see the car coming at him, but, unlike her, was unable to leap so instinctively to the curb. He died in the hospital: she remembers vividly the car's shining bumper coming toward her and, then, being somehow on the far curb looking back.

In a city of millions, on an island less than a mile wide, karma pursues one with alacrity. One keeps moving.

New York City is a city of survivors. The lions at the main New York Public Library entrance on Fifth Avenue are called Patience and Fortitude. Lives blow

through the streets like rumpled bits of paper.
Stories cancel each other out in an explosion of gun-
powder.

Gloria says on the East Side they talk about furniture and on the West Side they talk about the cin-
ema, and downtown they talk about each other. New
York City is in many ways a quintessential night city.
All of its major landmarks are buildings at their best
when they are underlit at night. New Yorkers at
night feel the city is theirs in a way that it never is by
day. The commuters drive out the Long Island Ex-
pressway or through the downtown tunnels or across
the George Washington Bridge and by seven in the
evening are gone. It is then that the town reverts to
its natives.

The performance at the theatre is not remarkable.
As the Indian Whore, Gloria gets to do some redskin
schtick, but little else. There is some extra humor in
the evening, because the director's remarks back-
stage at the interval are by mistake broadcast
through the lobby speaker, and the audience is suddenly listening in on what sounds like a half-time
pep talk, rendered in precise British speech.

The curtain is down before eleven, and Gloria
takes a container of yoghurt from the company refrigerator and eats it while she is changing out of her
costume and sponging off the paint. She uses a special base; Texas Dirt makes her break out. Back-
stage, in their dressing rooms, the men and women
of the company yell across to one another, still exhil-
arated by their own sense of performance. Parents

and friends filter back and stand about awkwardly,
unsure of how to congratulate the men in un-
dershirts and the women with cold cream on their
faces.

The younger men are singing Elvis Presley songs
in the shower. There is a game of double solitaire
laid out and interrupted, on a long wooden table.
There are coffee cups everywhere, which the costume girl keeps throwing in a bin as she passes, with
a hand and arm already encumbered by a dozen
hooped skirts. She yells into the shower for the men
to bring out their towels. The call for the next performance on Thursday is a half-hour earlier than
anyone has expected and there is general complaint.
A man who has played a clergyman in the evening's
second play is greeted by a woman in a long brown
cape, who kisses him loudly on the forehead. The
mother of the girl who has played the Queen of the
May complains that they wouldn't let her wait up-
stairs. She has a Southern accent, a gentlewoman
among less-than-gentle folk. Her eyebrows arch as
she surveys the room: the men running back to their
dressing rooms in towels, the women laughing
loudly together, the director in a black velvet suit
moving about like an agitated but imperial shore-
bird.

Gradually, the large central room empties, the
women going out in boots and long skirts, the men
in blue jeans. An actor from Fiji marches out in a
trench coat and cap; the Queen of the May wears a
black dress and a flowered shawl. She is fresh-faced
and beautiful without makeup as she stands calming
her mother, introducing her to whoever passes.

Gloria says good night to the dresser and the director and hurries out to Broadway to hail a taxi.

Gloria remembers a man called Moondog who used to stand in the cold along Sixth Avenue and wait for people to buy his sheet music. He was blind and dressed in fur in the wintertime, and he was perhaps forty, perhaps fifty. His hair was grey and his features were craggy, classic Scandinavian, and if one stopped to talk with him on a windy night, or maybe even buy a bit of sheet music, one was always surprised at how handsome he was. His moustache was long and unkempt, and there was often ice in it. He was a composer.

Gloria always looks for him when she passes Sixth Avenue, but he seems to have disappeared in the last year or so. She still presses her face against the taxi window as it drives south, for just an instant.

The Shiraz is a walk-up club in the Village. The lights are red and the red-flocked wallpaper in the long main room is lit with blue and gold sconces. The orange-haired hostess, a young woman from Athens, sits at a table off to the side of the entrance door. She is the wife of the owner, a Persian. She leans with one elbow on the table and smiles thinly as Gloria walks in. The room is large and L-shaped, with red tablecloths spread over a dozen tables. A three-piece band is warming up onstage at the far end of the room, and couples and groups are finishing their shishleek and babaganoosh, and moving on to the baklava. Gloria disappears into the curtained room behind the stage, after saying hello to the band. As they establish their melody, the men on the stand settle into a weaving lyric rhythm. This group is three pieces; usually she dances to four instruments: drum, violin, kanoon, and oud. Two of the men are wearing knit shirts open at the neck, and the man on the oud wears a necktie. There is smoke in the air and a heavy sweet smell of raisins and coriander.

When Gloria appears, the spotlight picks her up in a flash of bluish white. Her costume is made up of black and red scarves and a hundred tiny mirrors sewn over the fabric. On her fingers she wears a pair of zils, small cymbals which she strikes together for emphasis as she moves about the stage. She does a series of twirls, turning her body in quick rotations. After a few minutes the black veil is removed—then the red a moment later. She stops with out-thrust hip as a kanoon string is plucked and held quivering, then she turns again and moves about the stage with the red scarf held above her head. Her black hair catches the spotlight and reflects in bluish glints; her flesh is a cool pink, like ice cream.

The band accelerates its rhythm.

The Stomach takes over. Abdominal muscles mesh and pull apart; under the layer of soft skin, rippling sinew expands and contracts. Her hips toss the sequins and mirrors and layers of gauze about as she dances, like Birds of Paradise on speed.

The people at their tables applaud loudly; the band behind her suddenly cuts its metre in half and she is down on the floor, swaying back and forth under the light, every gesture describing a circle in the air, her hands taking over the focus. The rhythm increases, and she moves down off the stage and out among the tables, the light following her. Her hands move through her hair, her breasts and hips bouncing in a pattern that repeats itself over and over again as she circles the stage. Her stomach, her navel, her belly: the focus now for all the music, for all the prescribed motions. She returns to the stage and accelerates to a zil-punctuated finale. There is a final explosion, one last burst of sparklers, and she is done.

She exits through the crowd, and disappears again behind the dressing-room curtain. Some of the men call her back, and one stands with a bill in his hand, wanting to stash it in her costume, as is the custom in many clubs. Gloria doesn't reappear; she is only the first half of the show, and she has worked hard enough. There is always a hassle about what money belongs to her and what to the management, and tonight is not a charity event. The applause dies, and she stands in the dressing room for a moment, gently kneading her muscles, coming down from the scale of intensity under the lights. The singer-comedian comes on not long thereafter.

In clubs like the Shiraz, Gloria trusts her sense of self-preservation when it comes to having or not having a drink with the customers. In the city, after midnight, she listens for an inner voice whenever she is confronted by romance-minded strangers. If anything alerts her, she passes. Tonight there are no strangers, only friends, and friends of friends; a

young Persian she knows hands her a glass of tonic
as she walks by the bar. She has managed to acquire
quite a few Arab friends in the clubs of the city; they
like the fact that she doesn't drink. Her body, their
religion: same difference.

She also finds that alcohol dulls her intuition. She
occasionally takes a drink, though, just to keep herself from getting too rigid. She prefers hashish, but
finds that during the time of month she's most subject to cramps, a little cream sherry is most soothing.
She listens to her body. She has to. Her body always
seems to know when it's going to be a cold winter.

While she is finishing her tonic, the owner's wife
comes over to tell her that she is wanted on the telephone. She picks up the receiver next to the check-
room and recognizes the voice of her friend Rosalind. She turns her back to the sound of the band
and the couples who have gotten up to dance. A
man in maroon slacks and a pink shirt has taken off
his tie and twirls it around his head as he dances
with his partner. A stout woman in eyeglasses and an
ebony beehive hair-do gets up to dance alone, then is
pulled back to her table. The band is sweating, and
the air is blue with smoke.

Gloria has to raise her voice in order for her
friend to hear her.

"I know it's hardly past one, dear. Yes, you do
always know. But I'm not sure I'm up to it."

Her friend Rosalind has quite a few toney friends
and now wants Gloria to join the party she is with at
a restaurant, before they all go on to Le Club for
some late dancing.

"The king of what?" Gloria asks. "Well, of course I do, my love. Except I'm not really dressed for royalty."

As it happens, the party to which Gloria is invited is a royal party, a European king and his small entourage making a tour of New York. Rosalind and the king are old friends.

"What does he look like? I've only seen his face on a stamp. Really." She takes her mirror out of her shoulder bag and again studies her reflection while she speaks. "I *am* a wreck, and I'm *only* coming to help you out . . . but I'll be there in twenty minutes."

After hanging up, she has a moment's pause, because after the taxis and the herbs, she has barely enough for her fare home. Still, Rosalind is always flush: she'll borrow a ten from her on the way from the restaurant to the club. It will work out.

She fastens the scarf around her neck at the collar and says good night to the men at the bar. The young Persian is unhappy to see her go. But cognac with a king? It doesn't happen every night. She kisses him lightly on the cheek and then is gone.

Outside, on the landing, she digs through her bag just to see if perhaps she's stuck some money in a side compartment or in among her plastic bottles of pills. She hasn't. Money tends to evaporate like dew from Gloria's pale hands. It won't stay in her purse. When she has it she spends it, so she doesn't have it most of the time.

She hails a cab going uptown at Sixth. After she

pulls the door shut behind her, she hesitates before giving the driver her destination, which is uptown through the Park, off Central Park West. Perhaps she'd do better to go home and not have drinks with anyone at all. She should learn her lines. She should think about Nina. It's already been quite a full night.

Then, because she is Gloria, and because the actress is narrowing her eyes at the belly-dancer, the person who represents them both abruptly tells the driver to take her to the Café des Artistes. And he does.

When the cab pulls up in front of the restaurant, it has begun to rain again. A gentleman on the curb opens the door for her, and she cannot resist the gesture and tells the driver to keep the change. It's all she has.

The driver, a man in his fifties who has, at some point, put contact paper on the partition between front and back seats of his cab, turns around to watch Gloria as she passes through the glass doors of the Café. Now who the hell is that? he asks himself. He tries to place her in his mind and memory for half a block, but when he gets to Columbus Avenue going downtown, he picks up a fare who wants to go to the Chelsea Hotel, and Gloria vanishes from his ken, unplaced.

Inside the restaurant the waiters in their black vests and white shirtsleeves are already draining the central ice bowl at the long pastry table, and there are only five or six tables still filled. There is some hubbub about the table where a party of a dozen people sit drinking cognac and coffee, telling stories in French and English. Their laughing faces are caught and duplicated in the mirrored walls of the place, their features animated alongside the murals of nymphs among lacy green foliage. The restaurant itself is like a glass cage on two levels; Gloria spots her friend Rosalind immediately on the first tier. She doesn't wait for the maître d' to escort her to the table but goes up directly.

At the table the men rise to their feet. Rosalind stands with her arm around Gloria, introducing her. The king sits with his back to the mirror and rises to shake her hand. He is young, and unexpectedly good-looking. His eyes are dark, and there is something about his chin that distinguishes him from the rest of his party. The rumor is that he is to be married in a few months' time; a bachelor king making the most of it, stopping at his apartment in the Waldorf Towers while he enjoys the stimulation of the most stimulating city in the world.

Rosalind laughs, throwing back her neck against the ruffles of the crimson blouse she is wearing. Rosalind is as pale as Gloria is dark; there are two other women at the table and five men, who speak in the king's language as well as in French and English. It takes Gloria only a few minutes to see where she fits in, and where she fits in is very high indeed.

Cognac is ordered, and Gloria, seizing a pause, begins a long and very funny story about an incident at a club in Trinidad, where she worked a few months before. As she talks she is aware of the king's gaze, though she makes it a point to tell the story to the table at large. Her story is a success, and the party is amused. Other stories tumble out, and Rosalind's head is thrown back repeatedly, her neck vibrating with laughter against the deep red.

A party arrives from Lincoln Center, their opera programs stuck in rhinestone bags and serge coat pockets. They have seen *Die Fledermaus,* and there is a lot of chuckling over the chambermaid's performance. They pass through the room and around the corner to the bar.

Gloria, facing the king and the mirror, is more than a little animated. As the royal head moves, forward to laugh, or back to whisper in the ear of the older man next to him, her head quickly moves in response. It is the movement of a peahen face to face with a peacock, crested head erect: stabbing, but at the same time tentative.

As more anecdotes and stories follow, more cognac is drunk, and Gloria, after some urging, has a glass or two herself. Her eyes shine.

Beyond the tables at the Café des Artistes, in the powder room of the restaurant, there is on the wall a print of a young girl, barely pubescent, standing on a chair holding open a cloak to reveal her total nakedness. A number of men in black stand around her. It is a period portrait; the men look as if they are members of some renowned academy.

The restaurant is closing. The group is moving on.

Gloria applies a bit of additional color to each cheek and touches up the fine edge of her red lips. When she returns to the table, all the party are on their feet. They are by now the last of the Café's customers. The owner smiles at them as they leave, looking at them closely through his thick glasses.

She steps into the waiting limousine. It is much larger than it appears from the outside, and the back seat smells of pipe tobacco and expensive leather. Gloria is in the process of pulling down the jump seats for the rest of the party when the rest of the party gets into another large car and drives off. The king alone gets in beside her after a few moments, and begins to tell her about his adventures during a summer he spent on a training ship in the Baltic Sea some years before. She is unable to ask about the rest of the party until they are halfway across the Park. As they pass the Bethesda Fountain, he takes her hand between his own.

His apartment in the Waldorf Towers is not over-furnished. The furniture is Louis XIV, the crystal is Waterford, and the carpets are soft and thick. There are two older women who hover in the background of the apartment; Gloria wonders if they are there to give security to any other female presence, to act as subtle lubricants to the evening's ease. There is a soft murmur of strings, and there are candles.

Gloria finds that the king is sweet, if intense. The king finds that at moments of passion, Gloria thrusts her face into profile. In front of the flickering wax lamps spaced along the marble mantel, the two bodies move against one another.

They leave the room, the king guiding her to the chamber beyond. There, an hour is spent in darkness.

There is a certain moment in the night that is shared by friends and lovers across the island of Manhattan. It is a moment of reinforcement, of thinking of each other's well-being in the thin slice of time before dawn breaks. A nightcap of sorts; a boost of spirits; a communal focus of love and hope and confidence. Gloria's friends think of her, and she thinks of them, and the night is given its demarcation. The tide of night retreats, and the wash of the day begins.

Across the city, the day is being claimed. A television comedian is getting up to go jogging in the Park, to begin his day by trotting past statues and busts festooned with red and black and green graffiti. A trucker is loading crates of cabbages by the light of flames and lanterns into his double van at Hunt's Point market in the Bronx. His gloves are wet and he pauses for a few moments to dry them over a drum fire. A woman in Astoria rises with her infant son. She takes the baby to her sister's house on 34th Street; then she boards the PATH commuter line to New Jersey, there to clean the houses of those whose houses are already very clean.

A middle-aged woman creeps home to her Third Avenue apartment at exactly 5:00 A.M. There, the man she lives with strikes her without a word squarely on the jaw. The walls are thin, and the man sleeping in the flat next door awakens with a cold start. He sees it is an hour earlier than his regular waking hour, and he curses aloud.

From the Royal Apartments Gloria looks down at the sparse line of grey traffic forming in the early light. She remarks to herself that life is for the moment quite lovely enough.

The king sleeps.

It is the moment to leave. She moves quickly, because she has a life to lead, and because she doesn't
want anything—not an awkward word, not a false
note of emotion—to ruin the memory of what has
occurred. It would perhaps have been nice if her
leave-taking were taken more notice of, were pro-
tested in some small way. As the Wife of Bath once
pointed out, the woman does like to be thanked.
Never mind.

She stands looking down at the street below, and
at the buildings to the north on Park Avenue. Below
her, the flags hanging out in front of the hotel snap
heavily in the wet wind. There is a dawn breeze, and
the lights in the other buildings in the sky flicker in
the moisture-laden air.

She has heard, somewhere, that candles burning
past dawn bring bad luck. She crosses from the window to the mantel to snuff them out. Standing in
front of the long tinted mirror, she dips out the
flames one by one. She moves back to the window
and holds her hand against the pane for a few minutes. Really, it was quite lovely enough.

Abruptly, she wonders what Rosalind will say; the
spell is broken. Turning from the window, she
presses her cool hand against the back of her neck.
Then she walks rapidly from the room.

On her way through the long corridor, she picks
up a small cloisonné bowl from a hall table, turning it
over to see if it is signed. It isn't. She replaces it with
a certain amount of disdain. The grey-haired man
from earlier in the night is asleep in a chair, his cigar
stub stuck between his well-manicured fingers. Not
many girls walk out on his majesty; the vigilance of

aides is seldom tested at this hour. In the long carpeted lobby outside the suite, a maid is carrying two
large bundles of linen, folded and wrapped in brown
paper, to the laundry room. She watches as Gloria
walks to the elevator; when the two women's eyes
meet, the maid smiles and after a moment Gloria
smiles, too.

The lobby is empty. Outside there is a fine rain
falling. On the street the morning is coming up, grey
from the Bronx, pink from Long Island. The air
quality for the day is said in the 6:00 A.M. news
rooms to be Acceptable. There is no taxi queue in
front of the hotel at this hour, and she walks west
across the street, the rising light behind her.

A young taxi driver, heading south along Park Avenue, sees her standing on the median strip at 50th
Street. He sees a good-looking woman, standing
alone. She is a model or an actress or a dancer or
something. He knows the type.

She smiles as she enters the cab, pulling her coat
around her in the back seat.

"Where you going, sister?"

As he asks the question, he turns around to get a
better look at her through the plexiglass divider. Not
bad. He slides open the door of the divider with his
left hand so she doesn't have to raise her voice to answer. He has an hour to go, and he hasn't yet made
his fare. She doesn't look like she'll be going very
far.

She pulls the lapels of her coat up around her
neck, and leans forward in the seat.

"Listen," she says, her voice low and confidential,

"I haven't got penny one. But I'm only going to West 10th Street, and I've got a story that's worth at least a trip to Brooklyn and back. How about it? It's only forty blocks and it's an awfully good story."

She perches expectantly on the seat. Her hands are poised for gesture, anxious to begin. She seems not to doubt for an instant that her offer will be taken.

The driver looks at her, incredulous. What a city, he thinks to himself—what an unbelievable city. He studies her face through the yellow glass. Her eyes are bright—even though they are rimmed with asterisks of mascara—and she is smiling slightly, her head tilted.

Outside, in the rain, after only a few seconds the red light turns green. The cab waits, then pulls smoothly away from the curb, heading south.

Inside, Gloria tells him her story, the story of the night.